THE END OF THE MODERNIST ERA IN ARTS AND ACADEMIA

This book identifies the—now moribund—Modernist spirit of the twentieth century, with its "make it new" attitude in the arts, and its tendency towards abstraction and the scientific process, as the impetus behind the academic structures of universities and museums, together with the development of discrete scholarly disciplines such as literary theory, sociology, and art history based on quasi-scientific principles. Arguing that the Modernist project is approaching exhaustion and that the insights that it has left to yield are approaching triviality, it explores the Modernist links between the arts and academic pursuits of the West—and their relationship with street protests—in the long twentieth century, considering what might follow this Modernist era. An examination of the broad cultural and intellectual—and now political—trends of our age, and their decline, *The End of the Modernist Era in Arts and Academia* will appeal to scholars and students of social theory, philosophy, literary studies, and cultural studies.

Bruce Fleming is Professor of English at the US Naval Academy. He is the author of *Running is Life: Transcending the Crisis of Modernity*, *Modernism and Its Discontents: Philosophical Problems of Twentieth-Century Literary Theory*, *Why Liberals and Conservatives Clash: A View from Annapolis*, and *What Literary Studies Could Be, and What It Is*, among other works.

CLASSICAL AND CONTEMPORARY SOCIAL THEORY

Classical and Contemporary Social Theory publishes rigorous scholarly work that re-discovers the relevance of social theory for contemporary times, demonstrating the enduring importance of theory for modern social issues. The series covers social theory in a broad sense, inviting contributions on both 'classical' and modern theory, thus encompassing sociology, without being confined to a single discipline. As such, work from across the social sciences is welcome, provided that volumes address the social context of particular issues, subjects, or figures and offer new understandings of social reality and the contribution of a theorist or school to our understanding of it.

The series considers significant new appraisals of established thinkers or schools, comparative works or contributions that discuss a particular social issue or phenomenon in relation to the work of specific theorists or theoretical approaches. Contributions are welcome that assess broad strands of thought within certain schools or across the work of a number of thinkers, but always with an eye toward contributing to contemporary understandings of social issues and contexts.

Series Editor:
Stjepan G. Mestrovic, Texas A&M University, USA

Titles in this series:

The End of the Modernist Era in Arts and Academia
Bruce Fleming

The Civilizing Process and the Past We Now Abhor
Slavery, Cat-Burning, and the Colonialism of Time
Bruce Fleming

Temporal Politics and Banal Culture
Before the Future
Peter Conlin

Revisiting Modernity and the Holocaust
Heritage, Dilemmas, Extensions
Edited by Jack Palmer and Dariusz Brzeziński

For more information about this series, please visit:
https://www.routledge.com/sociology/series/ASHSER1383

THE END OF THE MODERNIST ERA IN ARTS AND ACADEMIA

Bruce Fleming

LONDON AND NEW YORK

Cover Image: Courtesy of the author

First published 2022
by Routledge
4 Park Square, Milton Park, Abingdon, Oxon OX14 4RN

and by Routledge
605 Third Avenue, New York, NY 10158

Routledge is an imprint of the Taylor & Francis Group, an informa business

© 2022 Bruce Fleming

The right of Bruce Fleming to be identified as author of this work has been
asserted in accordance with sections 77 and 78 of the Copyright, Designs and
Patents Act 1988.

All rights reserved. No part of this book may be reprinted or reproduced or
utilised in any form or by any electronic, mechanical, or other means, now
known or hereafter invented, including photocopying and recording, or in any
information storage or retrieval system, without permission in writing from the
publishers.

Trademark notice: Product or corporate names may be trademarks or registered
trademarks, and are used only for identification and explanation without intent to
infringe.

British Library Cataloguing-in-Publication Data
A catalogue record for this book is available from the British Library

Library of Congress Cataloging-in-Publication Data
A catalog record has been requested for this book

ISBN: 978-1-032-10600-7 (hbk)
ISBN: 978-1-032-10917-6 (pbk)
ISBN: 978-1-003-21768-8 (ebk)

DOI: 10.4324/9781003217688

Typeset in Bembo
by Taylor & Francis Books

CONTENTS

PART I
What Hath Modernism Wrought?   **1**

  1 Beyond Romanticism   3

  2 Movements   11

  3 Why Modernism?   17

  4 Academia   24

  5 Museums   35

PART II
Abstraction   **43**

  6 Explanation   45

  7 Science Envy   53

  8 Offended? You Win!   60

  9 Life After Modernism   65

PART III
The Spectrum of Disciplines   **71**

  10 Personal and Impersonal   73

vi Contents

| 11 Fundamental Rules | 88 |
| 12 Verifiability | 103 |

PART IV
Words in the World **109**

13 Form Follows Function	111
14 The Cloud	120
15 Circumstances	133
16 What Is the Self?	139

| *Works Cited* | *145* |
| *Index* | *148* |

PART I

What Hath Modernism Wrought?

1

BEYOND ROMANTICISM

Modernism, the last century in Western intellectual history—which means the history of Western artists and intellectuals, a small percentage of the population—began sometime around the early 1900s with the rejection of the Romantic love of tumultuous events brought to dramatic conclusions by strong personalities on dark and stormy nights. Modernism was born when interest diminished in extraordinary and hence unrepresentative individuals, and increased in abstractions about people considered as if far away. Because individuals were primarily considered as constituent parts of patterns, there was a shift from the things represented to the process of representation, and to words and works considered as if they were the fundamental building blocks of the world. This is the perspective of artists and scholars, so Modernism was and is a movement of these, first the artists, and later the scholars, who dominate the institutions of academia and museums, the home territory of Modernism. Now, in the twenty-first century, we are in the last phase of this turn to abstraction, the heads-I-win-tails-you-lose insistence of special interest groups that we must change our words, not the world. Oppression is so deep-seated that not even attempts to take action will accomplish anything. Actions by individuals are not what's demanded, just the utterance of specific words. In this last phase of Modernism we have finally thrown away the key to what Fredric Jameson called "the prison-house of language" in his book of that name, that the Modernist era locked us into.[1] Yet its walls are only words, and we can simply walk through them to the world outside. That is what I propose here.

Romanticism was colored in such vivid hues that it frequently turned lurid and overheated. Modernism, by contrast, is cool and gray. Initially it was steel gray glinting with the energy of discovery, and now, in its declining years, it has become merely mousy. Modernism in its early years had its own austere beauty, but gradually its oomph escaped it; now it's a deflated balloon that nonetheless we still hold aloft in classrooms, journals, and conferences.

DOI: 10.4324/9781003217688-2

4 What Hath Modernism Wrought?

But think of the power of youthful Modernism! The shock of the new in Picasso, Braque, Stravinsky, Schoenberg, James Joyce, Virginia Woolf, Malevich, Goncharova, Proust, Gertrude Stein, Guillaume Apollinaire, and Robert Musil: those were the days! Amazing, the progression in painting as Mondrian's outlines of everyday objects grew stronger and then were refined into right-angled black lines and blocks of color! Follow as Kandinsky's stained-glass-like fairy tale landscapes and Murnau paintings turn into explosions of color with only an echo of objects! Admire the development of literary theory as a stand-alone discipline: Victor Shklovsky and the other Russians, the Anglo-American New Criticism, Structuralism, Semiotics, Jacques Derrida and then Michel Foucault, then the power of this theory as it replaces reading the literary works themselves, now called "texts," in countless college classrooms! Follow sociology with its quasi-scientific social structures determining individual behavior, building on Marx and Freud's focus on human-related abstractions to which the individual is irrelevant! Live the heyday of anthropology—fieldwork on "primitive" cultures where we Westerners arrive by ship or plane, observe the natives for a few months, and board the same Western transport to take us back to our universities where we report our interpretations of what we saw to the less adventurous folks back home! Puzzle over difficult literature that a professor has to explain to you! Focus on how words mean in countless philosophy classes and conferences! And all this the result of the Modernist switch to regarding people and their products not as individuals but as tiny constituent parts of larger wholes that begged to be arranged, categorized, and researched: the humanities and social sciences as academic disciplines are born. And so, we set to work researching, arranging, and categorizing. Twentieth century Intellect had triumphed over nineteenth century Feeling, Modernism over Romanticism. What bliss it was to be alive!

But that was then. The earlier movement of Romanticism came, and then it went. Modernism displaced the Romanticism that begat it, and now, inevitably, is also going. Indeed, it's all but gone, enervated but protected by the structural inertia of the institutions where it lodged and proliferated after the initial Modernist explosion of artists and writers. For although the content of Modernism is an abstraction from individuals, its initial efflorescence in the early twentieth century was created by individuals making individual-sized art like paintings and written words. And its last act is fueled by individuals purporting to articulate structures so fundamental that individual resistance to them merely proves the power of the structures in words. In fact, words come from people in specific circumstances for specific purposes; they have no intrinsic power if the person you're talking at walks away and leaves you talking to yourself.

For that matter, all trends that later gain traction as movements, whatever their content, are started by individuals. Individual thinkers and artists are like sailboats that can simply tack to the changing wind rather than battleships that can turn only slowly and with great difficulty. But once battleships set course, they keep going far longer and more ponderously than the sailboats. By mid-twentieth century, Modernist abstraction had taken over academia and contemporary art showcases, whose

Modernist presuppositions most people, not least of all their practitioners, now incorrectly assume are simply givens of these institutions, and frequently assume are shared by the world outside them. They're not, and the result is that an increasingly isolated priestly caste is left murmuring inside their temples while the common folk—which is to say, the rest of us—go about our lives outside.

In retrospect, it seems that academic Modernism, whose latest form is identity politics, was the path the earlier artistic Modernism was fated to take. Academia allowed professors to distance themselves from and analyze human actions and works under something like laboratory conditions, far away from the people who did or made them, turning the noisy jumble of the everyday into the ordered silent academic world of the twentieth century's data-driven human sciences and the study and theory of literature that replaced individual works as subjects. The belief that what reading books or considering the actions of people does is add to a sum of external knowledge is the Party Line of humanities and social sciences today. It is rigidly enforced by almost all the professors themselves as part of their self-image and the notion of their worth. Now, victimization studies insist that they alone are the only truth—having rejected the idea of objective truth that allowed other groups to carry on. This too is a power play, yet the people most nakedly thirsting after power accuse everyone but themselves of doing so.

Without the distanced point of view of Modernism, the academic humanities and social sciences could never have developed into ordered systems of study at all, disciplines where the given is the system itself as opposed to its content. Modernism made this systematization into disciplines possible, allowing machines that are run as their own ends, the point being the chugging machine rather than what it produces. And this means that as Modernism runs out of steam, as it is doing, these machines/disciplines themselves—not just their contents but the very structure of their thought that separated them off from other disciplines—will falter and run down as well.

We are at the end of the Modernist century. Roughly speaking, this was the twentieth. But because Modernism—which includes its descendants of Postmodernism and whatever Slough of Analytical Despond we find ourselves in nowadays—began in its earliest forms in the late nineteenth century and now is expiring well into the twenty-first, we can speak of a "long" twentieth century the way we speak of a "long" nineteenth century that lasted until World War I. Rather like Norma Desmond's views of movies in their alteration from silent to talkies in Billy Wilder's classic film *Sunset Boulevard*, Modernism started big and has become small. Back then, they had faces—or at least huge individual visions.

Now we have academia that, for example in literary studies, writes articles considering work X from the perspective of theorist Y, paying homage to the earlier considerations of comparable or identical pairings by academics A, B, and C, and presenting the result as "research" in the buzz phrases current at the time. This then appears in a journal that not even insiders read, or is read aloud in a monotone at a conference to a handful of other academics in an air-conditioned windowless room of a chain hotel, most of whom are only there because they are

6 What Hath Modernism Wrought?

awaiting their turn, after the current speaker has finished and been rewarded by a tepid and polite smattering of applause, to do the same. And the goal of speakers at the same conference the next year will to be to do the same, and the next, and the next, though over time the buzz phrases change. It doesn't add to a sum of knowledge—it's just individuals expressing their thoughts. There's nothing wrong with that, because who knows, a few people may find this interesting either to rebut or fuel their own thoughts. It's just that this is not part of an organized discipline, and it's unclear why universities should pay for it.

Or at least that's the way it was. In 2019, Covid-19 put an end to in-person conferences, as well as to many programs and even colleges, and to the hiring cycle for new professors that had dwindled to close to zero anyway because of lack of students. How long, the buzz of the plane ride and hotel paid for by one's institution, the thrill of a large city and the networking over drinks stripped from the Zoom versions of these presentations that are surely (at least to some degree) our future, would we put up with this? The hollowness of the whole enterprise became clear.

The Modernist era required for its birth a change of focus with respect to the individualistic Romanticism that preceded it and that was its progenitor. This alteration was not so much what we are accustomed to calling, after Thomas Kuhn, a "paradigm shift"—which sounds like one thing displacing another (Kuhn never says how this happens)—but more a pulling back from the same world as before, like looking at the whole mountain range on a topographical map rather than a single individual in front of a single Alp.

Modernism's new structures were neither needed by the Romantic era nor, had they by some fluke been proposed, likely to flourish in it. Academic Modernist structures were neither of the two positions that had coexisted as developed methodologies in Romanticism, namely personal expressions and their opposite, the impersonal world of science—impersonal even if it deals with things inside humans like diseases and corpuscles. People who produced considerations that tried to give big picture models for the whole world not based on science were understood to be versions of Romantic individuals (such as Hegel, Marx, or Freud): they could and did have followers, but their viewpoints and methods had not yet codified into academic disciplines that chugged away when fed raw material by individuals. (Think of the way the underground machines in Fritz Lang's *Metropolis* are kept running by an army of workers.) Modernism past its early years, once it became institutional rather than individual, connected these extremes on a scale with an impersonal middle that it proceeded to occupy.

Modernism came to be from a distanced view of people—but still a view of people, not the completely impersonal galaxies, diseases, and microbes that define science. But it did this out of what I call "science envy": it was the attempt to move the personal end of the scale closer to science, to adopt some of its attitudes, terminology, and methods, and to demand agreement on the basis that its conclusions had been proven as part of the objective world. (Nobody thought that, say, Hegel had proven his world-view to be correct; you either agreed or disagreed for personal reasons.) This quasi-scientific viewpoint of human beings produced the academic humanities and social sciences considered as disciplines with codified methodologies, that could lead, like science (at least in the Modernist conception), to increasing knowledge—rather than merely being a trading of subjective impressions or a belief-based system that demanded adherence. Science was unaffected by the Modernist era until the "disciplines" in the center of the scale grew powerful enough to try to take down science with the "gotcha" of pointing out its subjective element (which of course it has, being something done by individuals).

Even our contemporary post-post-Modernists, the identity politics people, insist that they alone speak Truth and thus are being objective. Because others can also put forth their subjective points of view as if objective, this leads to what, in politics, the right wing (echoing the left) came to call "alternative facts." (Left extremism and right extremism are shoots from the same Modernist tree.) I have my Truth, you have yours, but mine is truly True and yours isn't (?), or perhaps mine is Truer than yours—echoing Orwell in *Animal Farm*. If everybody can claim Truth because they want to, the claim loses its punch. As Hegel says at the beginning of *The Phenomenology of Spirit*, quoting a German proverb: at nighttime, all cats are black. The result is the patchwork of competing micro-kingdoms of identity theory that now swarm around us. The good news is that we can just walk away and let them fight it out. They didn't like the rational over-structure that was designed to mediate between individual disagreements—fine: let them deal with its absence. If every person claims kingship, there is going to be trouble.

In the process of its initial abstraction from the world, early artistic Modernism was linked to the world, because the abstraction had to be effected: that was the source of its power. Now, the abstraction long since accomplished, its descendants have left the world far behind. This is certainly true of what we call Postmodernism, the embrace of the fragmentary and transient as the logical rebellion against, and therefore next step past, Modernism's high-culture broad-reaching complexities (such as Joyce's *Ulysses*, the cubism of Braque, or Schoenberg past *Transfigured Night*). If Modernism linked to the world, Postmodernism links only to a previous movement.

The idea that no structure was the new structure, or that a random displacement of the usual order of things (installations in galleries of things we see every day outside! Dirt or rocks on museum floors! Fat in vitrines!) was intrinsically interesting, held our attention for a time as a response to the difficult and rigidly organized high Modernism of the early twentieth century. Yet as became clear, the problem with Postmodernism is that one displacement or lack of structure (or set of extreme personal associations unclear to all outside the artist) looks very much like any other, and all are one-shot tricks. Once you get the point, the work is exhausted: you don't sit and stare at it. Postmodernist objects aren't so much works as ideas, intended as sparks for discussion. So its apologists had to be constantly interposed between us and the work, explaining it all to us. And the explanation, while necessary to make the object meaningful, was almost always more interesting than the work. Art therefore became academic, things requiring explanation from

8 What Hath Modernism Wrought?

insiders rather than things to be perceived and sensed, and so lost its connection to everyday life.

Modernism began with an embarrassment of riches in intellectual capital, a fortune in ideas generated by its shift in focus to abstraction. By now, however, what was once a colossal hoard has been divided and subdivided through generational succession, proliferation of descendants, and family bickering, so that it has become ordinary, with smaller and more subdivided groups jockeying harder for less and less. Now what we see is just a lot of unimpressive people giving themselves airs, trying to carry on as best they know how but still trying to keep up appearances for the sake of the family name. And in its last act, Modernist formalism spills out of its natural home of academia and takes to the streets, to insist that only my point of view is valid—and your protestations only show how right I am. It's the ultimate Modernist victory of the view that the world is made of words, and contemporary social justice warriors are merely the last tired form of Modernism, not (as they see themselves) mad, bad, and dangerous to know. My structure of words is more powerful than your structure of words! This is scary only if we still accept the Modernist assumption that words make the world. Academic Modernism is coming to an end not just because of Covid-19, but because its intellectual capital was spent, with giants long gone and issues reduced to crumbs.

Some academics, to be sure, do think that (for example) reading and teaching literature doesn't lead to a body of knowledge, but instead serves at best to further the development of the individual as a person. And some professors will even admit (and how many more think to themselves?) that they are weary of hearing the same thing over and over at conferences. A number are also tired of reading the same badly written contortions in scholarly journals that always start with summarizing and usually praising in extravagant terms (X's brilliant insight, Y's groundbreaking analysis—and why not? Praise so that you will be praised) previous articles before sketching out their (usually trivial) differences with their predecessors. Some academics acknowledge as well that students, not just "research," matter too, if for no other reason than that they are the constant inflow from the world outside and hence a reality check each semester. Yet in the Modernist century that conceives of the humanities and social sciences as an amassing of objective knowledge, students are incidental, the works that could change their lives considered as nothing but so much raw material to be fed into theoretical machines whose handles the professors turn.

Of course, the blame for this, if blame there is rather than just sighing, belongs not, or at least not entirely, to those who see themselves doing "research" in the humanities and social sciences. That's what they were trained to do in graduate school by people who were similarly trained. In the Modernist century, that's just the way you did it. This push to ape science is what drove the trivialization of the considerations of people and their products: you have to write a dissertation on a tiny topic that you can cover completely. And that's how you apply for a job—as a specialist in a tiny sub-field, that more renowned departments want to have a smattering of all over the map. But they aren't really even in the same field, or on the same field. Instead, each is making a tiny bore across a vast terrain like so many moles, oblivious to each other.

You write your dissertation, for example, on Polish popular drama from 1930–32. Or the works of a specific Polish popular playwright in these years. Or one work (probably two or three to show development) by this author. In order to give this some sense of importance, you do so using concepts of a specific theoretician or theoreticians. With luck, you find someone before you who has failed to do X or Y in considering the same subject, and your contribution to knowledge is that you in fact do X or Y, or perhaps both. (You're the one who claims that not doing X or Y is a failure.) Or you are rescuing your author from undeserved oblivion caused (say) by gender or ethnic (or other) prejudice, and you are righting the wrong of this person having been "excluded from the narrative." If you are lucky, a university press publishes your book in revised form, with all the bowing and scraping to others taken out. The stronger or even more outrageous your claim, the better chance for publication you have: say that though your subject seemed to be pro-Z it was actually "subverting" Z, or that contrary to popular (?) belief, it expressed A or B instead. Or that this author had been silenced by the bad guys.

It's interesting to you, perhaps (if you're lucky—many humanities PhD students tire of their "research" before it produces a dissertation, and many who start never finish the degree). But if so, having anyone else care as much as you or even enough to read your book, presupposes the same degree of intense scrutiny you have devoted to the topic on the part of the reader of your interpretation/discovery (of course you present it as the latter and not the former)—which it almost never gets because you're the only one who has read all these things from this perspective. You present your claims at your job talks (if there are any), and if you are lucky, get a job. Then (if you're lucky) you get to teach a course in something related to your "research," but invariably more general—say Eastern European drama, for several years until the students dwindle to two or three and you teach something else. A handful of libraries buy your book (or a seminal article appears in a specialists' journal nobody reads) and nobody checks it out.

This is a life? Still, it's what you were told a professor does. And you're one of the lucky ones to have gotten a job at all! (Your attitude is probably different if you're waiting tables instead.) If you got disillusioned along the way, you didn't even finish graduate school. Most people who powered through and finished found themselves (a) without a tenure track job, certainly not one at the level of institution where they learned how to turn the prayer wheel of humanities and social science "research" and/or (b) stuck in the boonies with uninterested students and growing harassment from administrators whose only concern, besides keeping the students happy, is the financial bottom line (these two goals overlap) and/or (c) failing to get tenure because someone in the department doesn't approve of them, and so out on the street at 40. What else can a PhD do? They look for re-tread programs, along with everyone else in their situation. They ask, along with Peggy Lee: Is that all there is? Maybe they should have looked ahead and asked earlier.

The Modernist disciplines are a vast network of machines that grind away and make a lot of noise to produce, with great effort, a pile of widgets that nobody knows what to do with, so they are catalogued and put on shelves. Now the machine is cranking out this: If I feel "marginalized," I rule. This may be exciting for groups that think that asserting their primacy makes them important, but it's merely fatiguing—because predictable—for everyone else. More fundamentally, asserting lesser status as something to be aggrieved about merely reaffirms the greater status of the group against which they are lesser. Being in opposition is a very comforting position, but if the government falls, the guerillas have nothing to rebel against. Besides, the various splinter groups aren't united merely because they are splinter. And the ultimate joke is that the majority group doesn't see itself as a group at all, instead as a collection of individuals. Thus the groups attacking the majority have to convince the majority that their understanding of themselves is totally wrong—while of course the understanding of the attacking groups of themselves is completely and by definition right. So more words, words, words, talk, talk, talk. And only those in the Modernist bubble think talk and words is all there is.

The dreary repetitiveness and relentless triviality of current academia and art is one (high) price we pay for the continued existence of exhausted Modernism. But the even higher price we pay is the dereliction of duty on the part of academics towards those who don't deal in these things professionally. Philosophy professors, to take one obvious example, write for the rapidly diminishing number of other philosophy professors and the even more rapidly diminishing numbers of philosophy graduate students rather than for non-professionals, who might benefit by some distance from their everyday situation. This leaves for most people a void filled, for better or worse, by advice columnists, self-help authors, television personalities, and social media influencers. Modernist-dominated academic philosophy is irrelevant to their lives, apparently proud of being so pointless. And art works could actually touch and enlighten people, not just play tag with other art works.

Note

1 Jameson, *The Prison-House of Language*.

2

MOVEMENTS

The history of ideas, regarded only as a series of concerns general enough to register from the perspective of years or centuries, consists of a series of questions that arise at specific times and places, catch fire and then, after variable periods of time, burn out. Every dog has its day, and the ideas that seem so fresh today will seem shopworn tomorrow. Or the day after, or the day after that; we can't say. Even given that the concepts that take hold—and most don't, beyond a few adherents—peter out at some point, it is difficult if not impossible to say beforehand when this will be. Nowadays everything is held to be a "social construction," but this notion too is doomed to obsolescence at some point—and this one is especially monotonous. Remember when the chic philosophy was existentialism? The chic literary theory Structuralism? Even Derridean deconstruction has perhaps finally breathed its last, and Clifford Geertz-style "let them tell their own story" anthropology is no longer so cool.[1]

These are things that we express, that interest us, and that we promote. Yet no historian of ideas has been able to explain how these intellectual fads roar up and spread or why they peter out and die, as all that initially catch fire do, and as our current one ultimately will. This is so since we are conceiving of them as beads on a necklace. Because ideas come from people, our concentrating on the ideas and not the people means we can't explain them.

Weber proposed what he thought produced the spirit of capitalism, namely a general change in people's religious spirit.[2] But he couldn't explain what produced this: he could go one level back, but not two. What produced capitalism, in his view, was, famously, the rise of Calvinism with its bleak view of predestination that split human action from what had been the goal of people in the Middle Ages, namely salvation after death. If we couldn't earn this or get it as a gift (the latter the Catholic view)—if our salvation or not was determined before our birth, albeit unknown to us—we might as well live life in a methodical fashion and devote

DOI: 10.4324/9781003217688-3

12 What Hath Modernism Wrought?

ourselves to sober work. Or is this "kid ourselves that" rather than "might as well"? The logic seems a bit iffy, perhaps for them as well as for us. The idea seems to be that we are trying to convince both ourselves and others that we are among the elect, while knowing that we can never actually know whether we are. Isn't that a little bit of a stretch? Apparently for them as well as for us, since according to Weber the habits of work and acquisition eventually lost their theological basis entirely and became ends in themselves. So religion caused economics. But what caused the change of religious outlook? How this could happen he doesn't say.

This is a problem with all explanations using general human causes for general human effects. What caused the change in the cause that produced the effect? We have to find the genesis of general change where it started, with possibly random notions of individuals coming from what I call the cloud behind words. Individuals are the genesis of ideas, though the degree of their spread outwards is the result of many factors. Why did popular ideas become so? That is a legitimate concern of historians of ideas.

Explaining abstract ideas by abstract ideas does not, in any case, work. Thinkers that give non-human explanations for changes of ideas have an easier time of it. William McNeill, for example, suggests in *Plagues and Peoples* that the spread of the plague in China and Europe in multiple infestations led to greater popularity of religions that emphasized suffering and resignation, such as Christianity and Buddhism (110).[3] We're not responsible for the plague, though we may be responsible for its propagation (travel and war are two of McNeill's usual explanations for the propagation of microbes), so this seems plausible. But problems with human explanations don't go away entirely. What isn't clear is why this didn't have the opposite effect instead, the reaction chronicled in Bocaccio's *Decameron* where some people had wild parties: carpe diem, Mardi Gras all the time. Why bother saving it up if you're going to lose it anyway? And Weber can't explain, similarly, why an inability to have any confidence at all in salvation would have led to frugal living and hard work rather than the opposite of devil-may-care waste.

Weber's logic, as well as the logic of all explainers of human ideological alteration, only works backwards. It takes what happened as a given; it doesn't predict. Weber sees that Protestant countries did better economically and suggests a way to explain this. But if he'd started with the Protestant creeds and tried to predict the future, he wouldn't have been able to predict the outcome that in fact ensued. So was this the explanation, or even the primary explanation? We can't say. McNeill starts with the spread of Christianity and Buddhism, and so on: the argument isn't that microbes had to have this effect on particular religions, just that this is a plausible cause of something that did happen.

Historians of ideas almost invariably make what we could call a Newtonian assumption: things continue as they are until something changes them. The continuation doesn't require explanation, but the alteration does. For example, in the Middle Ages, the concern of the vast majority of people was their salvation after death. We don't typically ask why this was so, only why it ceased to be so with the Modern Age. Nor do we ask how this was conceived by them, given that they didn't actually see death, or beyond it. What does it mean to see beyond the edge of the visible? In his *Tractatus*, Wittgenstein said we couldn't. But of course it could be made visible in words and images, the same way we can visualize the effects of our actions if we do X or Y, or tomorrow, or ten years from now.

So do they see only the words and images, or the conception of the thing itself? And why would this cause them to act as they did? If we conceive of ourselves as being, at 20, a fourth of the way along life's journey, are we imagining a sort of line divided into four equal parts and us positioned at the end of the first one? How and why does visualization of time left to complete a task help us work faster (or slower)? What does it mean to focus on something like our salvation (it isn't literally "focus"), or to make it the goal of our lives (it isn't literally a goal post at the end of the football field)? How does the visual image, if there is one, translate to action?

We can't actually explain human change in general, or continuity either—just in the particular, and usually not even then. Why did people (to use the USA of the last half century as an example) think the Pet Rock was such a cute idea? The Cabbage Patch doll with its "adoption" certificate? The fidget spinner? We simply accept that these things come and go, as we accept that we are interested in certain people or foods or places or authors until we aren't. I'm over him/her/that, we say. Or: I've moved on. Or: I got tired of it. Maybe we can try to explain why after the fact (his snoring suddenly got on my nerves! Her constant nagging eventually drove me crazy!), but we can't explain why this fact caused our reaction, or at this particular time. It just did.

Similarly, we can't say why literary scholars grew tired of, say, Structuralism. Was it because the young wanted to do something different than the old? Because the novelty of the ideas wore off as they devolved into largely mechanical applications to specific examples? Fads in, say, literary theory with their perhaps 10–20-year life spans are more transitory than the change that brought about the Modern Age, still with us after perhaps 250 years, or Modernism, dying after a century. Pet Rocks or the mini-skirt or maxi-coat are more transitory still. The fact that they are all on the same scale doesn't mean they are identical, and we're only surprised at transience at the more longer-lived end of the scale, what we call science and metaphysics, not at the end where the turnover is constant.

Explanations of the trajectory of ideas can't be reproduced and so can't be proven, as laboratory experiments can be. They can just seem more or less plausible. That makes sense, we say. Or that isn't convincing. Another person who comes along, perhaps years after our death, may offer a more convincing explanation. And so (to echo Kurt Vonnegut) it goes.

Ideas can't explain ideas, only things outside of humans, and this to a limited extent. Did the Roman Empire fall because of the decadent morals of its ruling class (Gibbon)? It seems plausible, but we will never know because we can't run it all again and change that one factor. Did disease foster Christianity (McNeill's suggestion)? Encourage it? Make it possible? How about this: plausible? Likely? We can argue any of these if we find inklings that this was so. However, we do know

14 What Hath Modernism Wrought?

that chemical element X reacts in such and such a way—always, insofar as we can tell (maybe in vacuum chambers not, or at very fast speeds, or at very cold temperatures? Maybe we haven't tested those yet or don't even know about them). In a laboratory, that is, a place that successfully eliminates all the things that in the real world can prevent this from happening, it's certain—or as certain as we can be given the state of things we have thought of—but only at this level of abstraction from reality. Put it back into reality and who knows what might interfere: weather? Contamination? And the laboratory itself is already in reality: the laboratory worker being drunk or inattentive could certainly change things too.

So how can we consider ideas if causality by human factors is an endless regress (people thinking X caused people thinking Y but what caused people to think X?) and causality by non-human factors is at best iffy? Here I am concerned with another way of considering how words and concepts come to be from the self. Creating them changes the world. This world change is Foucault's point that (in his most famous example) homosexuality didn't have a label and homosexuals weren't a type of person until they were identified with a word.[4] Foucault focused on the change in the world; I am focusing on the fact that something precedes and is presupposed by the use and invention of these words in this context. He is interested in after; I am interested in before. And there has to be a before, precisely because otherwise there is no way to explain why people think and say what they think and say, or why these change.

Foucault has given the creation of labels and categories a bad name because his interest was in questioning the negative valence for groups he wished to defend.[5] But not all labels are negative. We create new terms all the time: that's what science is about, and we do it elsewhere as well. If something is deemed another "society" or "culture" or "group" or "sub-culture," this is an attempt to position something. We sense that they are different, and so invent the notion of a society or culture to express this. Their valence can be anything on the scale from positive to negative.

Foucault has made it seem as if we constantly harden our concepts into absolutes: a man who once would merely have had sex with men "is" now "a homosexual." But we can also create concepts that are less absolute to replace more absolute ones. Using "skin color" to denote differences between people rather than "race" is something we do when for whatever reason we are no longer comfortable with the degree of difference implied by "race" between groups of people. We can even deny that they are groups at all, any more than orange cats are different from spotted cats—yet Doberman dogs are, we maintain, still a different "breed" from chihuahuas. That's because we have no incentive to obscure these doggy distinctions, and there is a whole history and economic structure focusing on the "pure-bred" nature of specific dog types.

Labels can go in either direction, towards more absolute or more relative. The Spaniards in South America developed a sophisticated nomenclature to specify the outcome of various racial pairings (the issue of white and Indian is one thing, the issue of Indian and black is another, the issue of black and white is yet another, the issue of any of these three with various others are other terms completely). For a time in the US, there were only two possibilities, black and white, following the "one drop" rule where anything other than completely white was black (whereas the French world allowed the possibility of métis, mixed race); now the US nomenclature is fragmenting again with "mixed race" and of course "Hispanic," whose meaning is yet to be defined—a language definition? A skin-color definition?

This conceiving of movements or periods as separated from individuals is itself a Modernist point of view. Rather than being the results of people, thought patterns are seen as abstract entities. So of course we have no way of explaining them. If, comparably, we give abstracted labels to two positions of the cat, say in and out, or asleep and awake, and do not consider the cat as an agent, we can only graph these variations, not explain them. All explanations have to be offered in terms other than the abstractions for which we are seeking explanations. However, we do have ways of explaining why lots of individual people get tired of saying X and start saying Y—but each explanation is particular and subject to revision. It's not as if we are predicting the future, after all: we are merely trying to explain the past. The bottom line is clear and is not determined by our back and forth about what caused it. The past isn't going to change because we argue about what caused it, so we can take our time.

It's not, as Brunetière thought, that movements or genres are living entities that have a natural life span we can predict.[6] Movements are nothing but the sum of the individual people who share common ideas or preoccupations. Many individuals can be receptive to the same ideas for reasons outside people—but the movements themselves cannot be the explanation for the fact that individuals think that way. We don't know how long movements will last, and some points of view never turn into movements at all.

People apparently take up ideas as a result of various events in the world around them—at least, seen in hindsight—and explanations are always after the fact, so this is a form of historical conjecture. War breaks out. Or there is an economic downturn. Or people are simply tired of older ideas because these have been around too long. The causes can be more or less sudden, more or less general—and it's only later that we can begin to argue about what these causes might have been; perhaps we never decide. In the middle of the Covid-19 pandemic, people talked of little else but that, and were re-reading Albert Camus's *La Peste* or Daniel Defoe's *Journal of the Plague Year*. We can't say yet what this time will add to intellectual history. Movements, like viruses, are spread from person to person, they don't exist or think for themselves. But we can say when both are booming, and sense when they are on the wane. And of course we humans are the reason they wax or wane.

Thus I provide a way to answer the question left both unposed and unanswered by thinkers like Thomas Kuhn, who famously threw up his hands and spoke in almost passive voice of "paradigm shifts," and Foucault, who traced our contemporary mania for labeling things to the shift in thinking that produced the

Modern Age without being able to say what caused this shift. Why does one way of thinking give way to another? In fact, the way the question is posed, and the presuppositions behind it, make it unanswerable; we have to re-fashion the question. We have conceived of "movements" or "paradigms" or (Foucault) "epochés" as self-subsistent entities unlinked to individual people, so of course we can't explain why they change, given that in fact they are the shorthand sum of many individuals with similar ideas.

Explaining "paradigm shifts" after the fact is possible, but only if we cease thinking the paradigm has any substance. Instead, we must look to see what in the world influenced people to think as they did. We have to explain a way of thinking in terms that are not themselves connected to thought. Similarly, the only way we can explain why one plastic jug of milk in the store has a blue cap and another a yellow is in terms outside the difference of color. The reason is likely to be linked to the contents: one jug contains skim milk, say. And this consideration of conditions of life is the terrain of history and sociology, which, rather than being that of a science that can approach certainty, is where we have an ongoing discussion about possibles and plausibles.

It's like explaining fashion changes. Why did men stop wearing codpieces? Why the eclipse of red-heeled men's shoes and stockings? There are possible answers, and they all have to do with the way individuals relate to the world. The fall of the *ancien régime*? The French Revolution? The Industrial Revolution? Plausible answers all share the quality that they use real world explanations for "paradigms." People think in similar ways—lots of people at about the same time—because of changes that have nothing to do with thought. If we stay in the realm of thought, we cannot by definition explain changes. All movements are nothing but amalgamations of individuals. So both Kuhn and Foucault were wrong to think ways of thinking ("paradigms") had existence as entities. They don't. Or perhaps rather, both were children of their Modernist time, taking for granted the abstractions others around them took for granted—and that we no longer have any reason to.

Notes

1 Geertz, *The Interpretation of Cultures*.
2 Weber, *The Protestant Ethic and the Spirit of Capitalism*.
3 McNeill, *Plagues and Peoples*.
4 Foucault, *History of Sexuality Vol. I: An Introduction*.
5 Foucault, *The Order of Things*.
6 Brunetière, *L'évolution des genres dans l'histoire de la littérature*.

3

WHY MODERNISM?

How did Modernism develop from its parent movement Romanticism? At best we can give only plausible answers to questions such as these, not scientifically provable ones—we're dealing with an alteration that only happened once, and so, that is not amenable to the codification and laboratory tests of science. After all, not everything is amenable to scientific consideration, just the things that can be abstracted from life and kept still long enough to study. And not everything either requires or allows a scientific explanation. Scientific explanations presuppose a specific limited sort of situation, and are the exceptions in life rather than the rule, which means that things that aren't scientific should stop trying to pretend they are.

Many thinkers, including M. H. Abrams in *The Mirror and the Lamp*, explained Romanticism as a rebellion against the Industrial Revolution and the rise of science. This seems plausible, but it only allows a movement to develop as long as other things than science still had confidence in their separate non-scientific natures. But after a time, this confidence, and hence the battle, was apparently lost. Science grew to seem unbeatable—confirm this by looking at its Victorian prestige for all but faith-based outliers—so Romanticism, a rebellion against it, grew weaker. Gradually, more and more people apparently decided to side with the victor, science. The apparent result was Modernism, that defines our time and that can be summed up in one phrase: science envy.

We can move beyond our now played-out Modernism by understanding that there are other undertakings than science. Science is a specific enterprise at only one end of a scale whose other end is the personal and individual. We need to regain our confidence in the individual as the measure of considerations of people rather than allow it to be used as a means to an end in the academic humanities and social sciences, created by and for Modernism. And in the arts, the initial Modernist act of abstraction from individuals behind us, art about art is no longer

DOI: 10.4324/9781003217688-4

18 What Hath Modernism Wrought?

compelling for anyone but a small number of insiders. We have to prevent science, important though it is, from acting as a magnet that pulls everything else in its direction. We need to end science envy and hence science creep—that we ourselves allowed and indeed encouraged in the age of Modernism.

This Modernist pulling back from a focus on a content of individuals to increased abstraction also meant that anything at all could be regularized and studied inside academia, since it was the method that provided the unity of the enterprise, rather than the object. Initially this meant, for example, expanding the scope of vision from a canon of classical texts and works to contemporary literature, then to local literatures (such as American)—and later in the century on beyond zebra to everything else, such as Barbie dolls and Princess Diana, Facebook and TikTok.

For insiders, those who developed the methodology and took it for granted, this expansion of purview of the machinery was inevitable (the machinery is the point, not what is fed into it, and indeed it requires feeding) and only positive: it meant they could study Pacific Islanders or American Literature, and later, inaugurate Queer or LatinX studies, then encourage considerations of the Internet and social media. This ceaseless expansion outwards of academic reach echoed the way capitalism, according to Marx, was condemned to perennial expansion to new markets, and hence to colonialism—and indeed was a sort of academic conquering of increasingly far-flung territories. Late Modernism, influenced by Foucault, held consideration of geographic Others to be a culpable act of oppression, and anthropology agreed, whereas the similar academic conquerings of domestic sub-territories such as Queer or LatinX studies were held to be an act of freedom and affirmation. The distinction is merely between whether it is "good guys" or "bad guys" doing the conquering and who gets the now almost non-existent professorships in the increasingly irrelevant institutions of academia, "us" or "them." From the perspective of the academy, these are identical, both being a methodology in search of new raw material. And the calcification of academic disciplines into accepted methodologies that all adherents had to follow was the result of this ceaseless expansion. New raw materials require established methodology to process them.

Traditional academics today bemoan the attack on the standard "canon" of Great Literature in the 1990s (vilified by its opponents as being the insider tracts of Dead White Males, mostly straight), the relentless "deconstructionist" attacks of the gleeful Derrideans of the last decades of the twentieth century, and now the transmogrification of Foucault's insistence, borrowing from Nietzsche, that there is no such thing as neutral intellectual curiosity: if you study me, it's to exercise your power over me and to stifle my voice! So hire me and I will speak for my group! A college hiring decision? What a trivial end. Still, for the few academic conservatives left standing, the biggest problem is the "identity politics" of our day: literature taught as the power tool of specific ethnic and gender/sexuality groups.

But identity politics is the last turn of the Modernist screw, late evidence of the century-old Modernist academic hunger for new worlds to conquer. The power

Why Modernism? **19**

play is by academics themselves, made more pointless by the fact that the humanities and social sciences in colleges and universities are hemorrhaging students and their departments hire almost no new faculty members, and their intellectual points become ever more trivial and repetitive.

It was an early response by an older generation to see those battering at the traditional academic gates as a real threat. Now it's clear there are no castle walls left to storm, and nobody inside. Sure, let them take over. They'll find empty rooms. Modernist academia doesn't need to be resisted: it dwindled away on its own, the victim of its own abstraction from the world, which is also the source of its success as academic disciplines. It expanded its territory, but its victory was Pyrrhic, because it turned out nobody but the conqueror was interested in this territory. It claimed victory over a land that turned out to have few natural resources and even fewer subjects. Why bother to defend it? The juice isn't worth the squeeze.

The identity politics of our day that has fragmented us into factions struggling for power is the last instantiation of Modernism, its logical end. Being horrified at its antics gives it far too much credit, not to mention no end of satisfaction to its sad little footsoldiers, convinced they are living at the beginning of an era rather than at the end. Let them attack each other. Nobody's listening anyway.

Didn't see that coming, did you? we say, somewhat sadly, to the dwindling next generation of Assistant Professors who found one of the almost non-existent tenure-track jobs teaching what once seemed so important back in graduate school, to be specialists in increasingly sub-divided and trivial slices of what is no longer even an entire pie. How long will it take for you to realize, unlike Rick in the movie *Casablanca* who said he came to Casablanca for the waters but claimed he was "misinformed," that you actually were misinformed? And who, or whom, is to blame? Your graduate school that used you to teach freshmen who paid multiples of your stipend to take courses for which you were paid peanuts? Your dissertation advisor who wasn't willing to admit that the Titanic was going down and all you were doing was rearranging the proverbial deckchairs? The System? God? Certainly not yourself for having been a sucker.

What those who celebrated the expansion of codifying methodology into uncharted academic territory emphasized was only one of its aspects, the greater reach of inclusion in their academic project, as if the academy existed to subsume everything under its aegis. In fact, this expansion of academic purview is related to the increasing calcification of academic disciplines. In order to expand the reach of a discipline's methodology, the methodology that was used in this expansion had to tighten and become uniform. For Modernist academia, this meant using common specialized vocabulary, though the point was that it was common to those inside the discipline, and specialized, not what it was at any given time. Those inside the discipline affirmed their insidership by keeping up with trends, repeating specific phrases and using specific tools like the latest in trendy fashion, until these were replaced by other repetitive vocabulary. The common methodology was the assumption that only whatever vocabulary was current among insiders

20 What Hath Modernism Wrought?

was what had to be used. This alone means that the humanities and social sciences were not adding to a common body of knowledge, but were merely the working out of subjective fads.

Thus the few outsiders who cared to listen in heard the same phrases used over and over until they were replaced by other phrases. Now everything for English professors, for example, is "problematized" and "interrogated." Or in the buzz phrase of the current generation, "Speaking as a member of marginalized group X or Y, I..." Academics in literature departments, to stay with my own field, will remember the use of many analytic tools over the last few decades that were all the rage until they weren't. First in the Modernist codification of the study of literature, there was "ambiguity" and "close reading" and the Metaphysical Poets (The New Criticism). Then there was everything seen as a system of signs or arranged in squares of opposing concepts (semiotics, structuralism). On this followed the enthusiastic use of French phrases from Derrida (deconstructionism) by largely monolingual English-speaking American academics, such as *mise en abîme* and *sous rature*. Then there was the craze for seeing everything through the lens of the quotational fragments of Walter Benjamin, his name pronounced in scholarly papers read at the North American Modern Language Association with a German accent, Valtah Benyameen (Postmodernism), even by those who otherwise spoke no German. Simultaneous with this was the insistence that all considerations of anything were an expression of power by those doing the considering (Foucault and his follower, Edward Said). The newest craze is seeing all works as emanations of racially defined groups (Marx would have said economic class—and there are Marxists too) and thus for prefacing every statement with "Speaking as a LatinX/ Gay (wo)man/trans-gender (wo)man, I..."

Because of the attempt to turn all enterprises involving people into something closer to science, Modernism neglected the individual point of view. At first this assertion may appear counter-intuitive, since the celebrated Modernist literary technique of "stream of consciousness"—for example in Arthur Schnitzler, Virginia Woolf, William Faulkner, and James Joyce—seems all about the individual. Yet this technique is not about showing life as lived, it's about fictional individuals rendered in the past. Living in the present, where we have some traction with the world—making it happen, rather than being whooshed along (as Woolf expressed it[1]), or by thrownness (Heidegger[2])—is quite different. (Sartre may have come the closest with his notion of absolute freedom—which of course we do not have, as we are confined by our circumstances. But perhaps his point was that we are always at a zero point at every moment: because we are particulars, abstractions can't say what we will do.) The outcome of the present can't be considered a given in reality, only on a surveillance video that can be repeatedly viewed, or in the laboratory, where conditions can be controlled, or on the page of a Modernist novel, where it's nailed down and has already happened, or where the particularity of it happening or not is irrelevant to the abstraction.

It's the particularity of the moment that we (at least partially) make happen that Modernism has neglected. We can get up close to look at the blades of grass on the

Why Modernism? **21**

lawn, or we can see a green carpet (or one that, troublingly, is not so green) from afar. Science sees the green carpet, and we can talk in its terms of fertilizer and watering. The Modernist humanities sees groupings or patches of grass. But in fact, each blade grows alone: some thrive, some die. The individual blades don't go away just because we don't pay attention to them.

The Modernists took works and words for granted and started considering them once they were born, so that they seem merely objective parts of the world to be analyzed. I, by contrast, consider the period of pregnancy, and even before. If I stop writing here and now, this essay doesn't exist. Whether or not this would be a loss for the world remains to be seen, but it is something I work out with the world, and the world with me. It's complicated, this relationship, but without me, whatever this entity is, none of it happens. Perhaps I am not an entity at all but a crossing of forces. What I am not is irrelevant, as Modernism makes me.

People produce words under specific circumstances from an individual pre-manifold I call the cloud behind words, and that I consider below. Ignoring the cloud as Modernism has done means that we have too abstract and apersonal an understanding of words, and thus get them wrong. But a further deleterious effect of ignoring the cloud is that doing so has allowed the creation of the caste of what we may call modern Scholastics, arguing to infinity over modern version of questions like how many angels can dance on the head of a pin. That's the way we caricature the Medieval Scholastic debate, at any rate, now that we have ceased to be interested in it (and this is how all debates end, rather than by anything actually being solved: we simply lose interest). But it makes perfect sense and is by no means this trivial if we enter into the mind-set of those who carried on the debate. Still, if most of us have moved on, this sub-group will be left stranded, as Modernism has increasingly been.

For consider: even an infinite number of angels lacks extension, which was the real issue way back when. They don't have material bodies—as we imagine them. But what do they have? What can we say about them? Do angels have gender? The Scholastics thought not. So is the Archangel Gabriel as much Gabriella as Gabriel? Are they simply beyond gender, not androgynous but simply without any position on a scale of gender (and what does this mean?)? Let's say we win the eternity lottery and are admitted to heaven. How can we recognize any connection between angels and people we knew, now stripped of gender of any sort, even imprecise, and presumably all other qualities (as we ourselves will be)—no longer tall or short, fat or thin, family or foreign? Do we or they have memories of life on Earth, knowledge of having been male/female, black/white, tall/short, subject of King X or citizen of a democracy? This question is especially puzzling as angels were all held to be the spirits of people as they were or would have been at age 33, the age Jesus is traditionally held to have been at H/his death, regardless of what age they died, from one minute to Methuselah's 969. Once upon a time, much hung on the answers to these questions that we have ceased to ask, and in fact find comical (cf. angels, dance; pin, head of). Inside this bubble, these questions are very important. Outside it, they disappear.

22 What Hath Modernism Wrought?

Modern Scholasticism makes sense inside its bubble and equally lacks importance outside of it. Nowadays we have literature professors who spend their time tracing the connections of a "text" with other "texts" rather than thinking about how their readers (usually young adults) can use them to understand the world. Or they claim to show how a "text" effected changes in the world on other continents when actually, politicians and soldiers did that. Or they claim that including a certain work in a course few students take will strike a blow for societal inclusion. We have artists who make works that refer to other works and to the concept of art itself, which interest only other artists; we have fashion designers who make clothes about other clothes, seeking to make statements about materials and garments rather than making serviceable and attractive body coverings for people outside this narrow world; we have scholars whose highest goal is to "interrogate" and "problematize" X or Y rather than linking these productively to the lives of anybody but other scholars. And what do they do with X or Y when it is problematized? Nothing. They have achieved their goal and walk away.

The problem with these is not that they are wrong, because they aren't. No focus is wrong, because it is merely a direction of attention. However, the focus is extremely narrow, and this is something that becomes clear as a result of its very success: we can see clearly what it isn't doing. Indeed, this fact is the reason why stating an idea clearly starts the clock ticking toward its death. Scholasticism wasn't wrong either; it's just that it became irrelevant because of people doing other things and thinking in different ways. So nothing is accomplished by these modern day Scholastics explaining again the questions of interest to them: people outside increasingly don't care. That is how all ideas die. We don't kill them, we just stop feeding them. Their keepers, of course, are attached to them, and so keep nursing them along. We can't win an argument against them, but we can do better than that: we can walk away. No argument is won; we just stop talking.

During the first surge of early Modernism, the general response was derision and rejection. D. H. Lawrence and Joyce had their books banned; Gertrude Stein was mocked; Hitler didn't have to encourage Germans too much to find the anti-beautiful works of the German Expressionists "Entartete Kunst"—art without an artistic essence, degenerate art. It was World War II that allowed the victory of Modernism and "degenerate art," as it seemed everything the West had fought for. Who would defend the Nazi sculptor Arno Breker after that, with his modern Greek nudes standing for Victory and the Army? The difficulty of Modernist art seemed an alternative both to the Nazis and the manufactured consumer goods that so repelled the Frankfurt School, fleeing to the US from Germany. If Hitler disliked it, it had to be good. And so the people who failed to profit from Modernism were silent. Now, 75 years after the end of World War II, people no longer feel the need to like what Hitler criticized. It doesn't do much for them either, plus it's over a century old. Ideas can't seem fresh forever, because they aren't.

How often can outsiders to the academic humanities and social sciences, or for that matter even insiders, hear the same tired bromides before these begin to seem trite? The answer, thankfully for the world if not for their purveyors, is: not forever. And this spells the end of Modernism: in codifying the previously variable individual, the academic version became too uniform and hence tiresome to all but its most entrenched practitioners. This is the source of the trivialization and desiccation, at least for outsiders, of the natural Modernist habitats of academia and the arts, which have turned into exercises for the initiated, a shrinking and increasingly irrelevant sub-set of the larger population.

Notes

1 Woolf, "A Mark on the Wall."
2 Heidegger, *Being and Time.*

4

ACADEMIA

The two largest institutions where the Modernist machinery once whirred and even now continues to turn, like a factory in East Germany propped up by the State and responding to no demand for these products as opposed to some products (nobody wanted a Trabant when they could, after the fall of the Berlin Wall, aspire to a Mercedes), are, first, contemporary art, which defines itself through and frequently against the gallery, the market, and museum; and second, the humanities and social science departments of colleges and universities, that exist only within the ivory tower and that are utterly irrelevant (and NB: not at all interesting, much less threatening) to those outside it. It was in the protected conditions of these institutions that the Modernist sensibility took root and took over. Now the academic disciplines that Modernist abstraction from individuals created grow endless tendrils like potatoes withering under their transformation into fruitless tangles symbolizing the mental deterioration of the heroine of Roman Polanski's *Repulsion*, in which Catherine Deneuve plays a hairdresser slowly going mad, her potatoes increasingly nothing but useless offshoots.

Colleges and universities are one natural home of the Modernist separation from the world outside of what insiders do, the assumption that abstraction is the only way to go. Yet even on college campuses there is increasing pushback to this orthodoxy because of a fundamental split between professors and students. Professors have bought into the Modernist orthodoxy; students (aside from a group of insiders in training) haven't. Business has become the most popular college major, and classes in the humanities and social sciences are disappearing. And why not? Our age at the end of Modernism is self-referential and circular, not to mention arid, at least inside the ivory tower of academia and museums. When it's not arid it's strident: I'm the professor and I'm here to show you what the correct reading of this subversive/identity-affirming text is! The student wonders: What if I see something else? I flunk the test. How am I going to graduate like that?

DOI: 10.4324/9781003217688-5

Each separable discipline of the social sciences and humanities in the early and mid-twentieth century was based on a single initial leap of abstraction that has come to be so taken for granted it is now openly attacked from within the discipline. The result is that each discipline preserves the outlines of the initial garment of its early years, but is now so full of holes it can no longer keep out the cold. All have been shredded to rags, yet professors still dutifully don (!) them, as if unaware of how useless they have become. There may still be a department of sociology or anthropology, French or Comparative Literature. But they are filled with people who now see that the initial leap that created them is untenable. These now largely attract people eager to further shred something that is so fragile the shredding is uninteresting to all but the most dedicated insiders, those who have (so to say) the moth's-eye view of the sweater of which they are trying to find enough remaining to consume. This is the victory of Modernist abstraction, and its logical end state.

In order to imagine itself a discipline, literary study, for example, had to take an initial leap into abstraction that left individual works far behind—first into the notion of a unified national whole, and then into the various notions outlined above, from Structuralism through Derrida and Foucault to works as the expressions of immigrant or racial groups in the West where they are minorities (this last was after having debunked the notion of a unity of national literatures and an attack on the notion of race; apparently minorities have coherence and unity that majorities lack). A similar leap was effected by all academic undertakings in order to form themselves into disciplines under the influence of Modernism.

The "discipline" of my PhD, comparative literature, was based on the Romantic (Goethe, Herder) notion that (say) French literature expressed a different spirit than German. But for the Romantics it wasn't a discipline, rather a point of departure for subjective judgments that the twentieth century found unpalatable. So in its Modernist abstractionist flowering (the 1950s–2020ish), comparative literature got theoretical, with the Yale-Hopkins deconstructionists adopting first Derrida (there is nothing outside the text, and I can show all the things this particular text leaves out—a rigorous maze of words) as their guru, then Foucault (words create power in the world, and always to control, so any words must be met with other words). And since then, comparative literature has given up comparing literatures, or even being necessarily about literature at all, and makes intellectual structures for the consumption of insiders (students and professors) of anything people want to throw in. Cultural Studies (Barbie and Princess Di)? Check. Facebook and TikTok? Check. Street dance and performance art? Depending on how liberal your department is, probably also check. And if they don't say OK, then another school, eager for students and feeding the machine of graduate students, will. Anything can be fed into the capacious maw of institutionalized disciplines.

But now (a) nobody with a PhD in comparative literature can get a job, (b) many universities have ceased giving these degrees, and (c) there is no clear definition of the discipline left. What are we comparing? And why? An acceptable comparative literature dissertation in my first graduate school back in the 1970s, I

26 What Hath Modernism Wrought?

was still being told, would be on one novel by Balzac (French) and another by Moravia (Italian), not Balzac and Sartre. Huh? We no longer believe a common spirit or essence links Balzac to Sartre but excludes Moravia, and Modernism became international anyway, with T. S. Eliot's closest progenitor probably the French poet Jules Laforgue, and Picasso borrowing from African sculpture. Now numerous European countries sit in the same parliament in Strasbourg and can have each other's contributions translated into English. And the idea of comparing equals is not the direction that so-called "post-colonial" studies has gone, where we excoriate the colonizer and talk up the colonized, assumed to have been in the weaker position.

Besides, literature may not matter at all, given the power of social media. Let's study that too! Nothing is left of the idea of comparative literature—now it's just a scholarly free-for-all that, because it claims things people use in daily life (like social media) as legitimate grist for its mill, is without even the claim of high cultural worth that a study of "great literary works" once had. Comparative literature as a "discipline" was based on abstracting from an initial conceptual distinction that has ceased to hold sway. Now it just means talking about anything we can separate out from the flow of human existence as products, from novels to Snapchat to Marina Abramovic hurting herself. If we can't separate it out, it can't be abstracted and so can't be woven into patterns of abstraction.

Considering two dances may not be accepted as comparative literature, nor the comparison of two schools of painting—but a dance and a painting linked by a theorist is likely to be. Doing this keeps professors (and graduate students) occupied, but it certainly isn't knowledge—just a kind of diary of intellectual curiosity. And who cares about that but you and the three other people in the world who share your interests? And all three of them want to show how you're wrong and they're right. Sure, meet them at the Modern Language Association if there will still continue to be one. But don't pretend what you're doing has any larger purpose than keeping you amused.

Literary studies in a single language? We have to have a unified entity of one language's "literature," which we no longer have. The whole departmental structure of the modern university, created during the heyday of Modernism, is now in disarray. Now we don't have an agreed upon list of works we are dissecting, just a series of competing candidates for attention. Why analyze this one rather than that one? The answer seems to be, we give the grease to the squeakiest wheel. Who yells loudest? This is personal, and anything but abstract. Modernism has shot its wad.

Other Modernist disciplines (as once they were) have similarly fragmented, and have similarly become about individuals pursuing their individual hobby-horses. Take psychology. Its great Modernist leap was the idea that we could arrive at truths about the way humans acted that were based on invariable structures of who we are as people. But this initial abstraction of all humans is unviable in our age of fragmentation. Every act of creating finer distinctions and smaller groups to generalize about trivializes the claims, and these smaller groups can themselves be

Academia **27**

fragmented into even smaller. The initial leap that created psychology has tripped over itself. And that means psychology lacks a foundation myth. We can continue to have a university department of "psychology," but that is a rubric that no longer unifies anything, least of all itself.

Sociology, another example, was based on the initial leap of postulating unified entities we baptized "societies" or "cultures." The leap was saying that there is at some Platonic level an entity sufficiently unified that we can cut it apart and analyze it. It's like dissecting a body rather than cutting into a mess of ball bearings on the table. The unity of the body is a necessary quality for its dissection and analysis. Only now, we no longer think the body is unified; all we see is a random arrangement of fragments. The big picture leap that made the discipline initially exciting is lost. Even words such as "culture" or "society" have fragmented and trivialized, and are used as the rough synonym for "perceived similarities," almost invariably negative. We speak of a "culture" of harassment in a television network or business, for example. Some academics speak of a "culture of rape" to mean the contemporary West where rape is rare (rather than, say, the Eastern Congo where soldiers routinely rape women as a tool of subjugation). And we don't assume a unified "society" at all, just an agon of competing groups.

Sociology is related to anthropology, another Modernist invention. This also presupposes coherent "cultures" that seem clearly unified because they are far away and look different from our own and seem isolated and self-sufficient: we go to them, they don't come to us. Now they do come to us, so anthropology is pointless. But seeing our own culture as unified almost always requires seeing it in terms of something Outside: for Thorstein Veblen in *The Theory of the Leisure Class*, it was the similarity between Gilded Age extravagance and the burning of valuables to impress in the potlatches of the Northwest Indians. Weber offered his contrast of religions in numerous works.[1] This is staying at home and offering the Outside as a reference point. If you actually go Outside and directly or implicitly compare what you see to what goes on at home by using concepts that link them (say, marriage or sexual customs), you are doing anthropology. Both require abstractions.

Anthropology's initial leap has ceased to seem viable, perhaps even more evidently so than that of sociology, because it presupposes even more clearly a power relationship we now reject. It's not in fact a relation of oppression, which is the claim of many people influenced by Foucault. It's the next step beyond that. In the power relation that produced anthropology, we're not fighting them, we're studying them, which assumes we're not afraid they will boil us in a pot and eat us when we go there—note, we go there, not the reverse. And the reason we're not afraid of them, nor are we establishing dominance, is that all this been settled. But we're not treating them as equals either, instead as quiescent or compliant subordinates. Precisely because outside isn't so Outside anymore, what with airplanes and social media, and they talk back to us in the colonial language, skyscrapers dot their cities and all have access to the Internet, there is virtually nothing left of the outlines of Otherness on which anthropology is based. Now we are busy defending not even the rights of formerly primitive people outside to tell their story

28 What Hath Modernism Wrought?

(which is one intellectual time zone back into the past, the Geertz alteration wrought upon of Malinowski/Margaret Mead anthropology) but of their right to be heard and indeed perhaps predominate in our own world. Interestingly, this means we have now gone back to the West-centric worldview before the Age of Exploration: we consider how they fit into us, not how we compare with each other.

The Modernist leap of abstraction postulating unified structures of people living together and defined as units by geography became possible at a certain time and now is impossible. The assumptions behind disciplines develop, and also weaken and die. Anthropology grew from and presupposed the way of interacting with what we now call Otherness that reached its flower in the Victorian Era, the age of colonization. The über-influential Foucault and his popularizer and disciple Said saw correctly that the possibility of academic study was the result of a specific power situation.[2] But being academics themselves, they flattered themselves that the power came from academics, that writing about Others was what cemented the Others' subordinate status. It's quite true that in order to study something, it has to sit still, and also not attack us. The first means that sociology and anthropology naturally assume that what they are studying is not shape-shifting as it is studied. We can change, but we are offended when they do. They need to sit still so we can study them! Anthropology, with its greater reliance on geography to unify the subject, naturally has a very strong predilection for objects of study that don't change over time: its subject matter is the whole culture. If they are fluid, there is no coherent object of study, as now has become the case. The second means it isn't a threat. And this is something institutions like armies determine, not academics.

Captain Cook didn't see "cultures" when he stopped at South Sea islands, but only potential trading partners or enemies. If settlers to North America were still fighting Indians (or First Peoples, as Canadians call them), there would be no National Museum of the American Indian on the National Mall in Washington, DC. What Foucault and Said and their academic epigones forgot is that we first had to have subordinated these outside "cultures" to even study them academically as "cultures." And that means not with words but with guns, and the army. It's not writers who make academic study possible—which is circular in any case. It's soldiers.

So Modernist abstraction comes as the next step after colonization for subjects like anthropology and sociology. We may get to feel we are treating them as equals, and feel good about ourselves, but this is only after we have eliminated any threat they had for us. The owl of Minerva, to co-opt Hegel, only flies over the battlefield when the shooting is done. It's a specific development at a specific time, which means that just as it hasn't been around forever, it won't be around forever. The idea of a "society" or "culture" requires us to see equally valid or at least substantial multiples of these, as we did for a time in the early twentieth century— much as the idea of forms of government requires us to see more than one, or the idea of scientific "paradigms" requires us to see more than one. If we know only one of something, we don't go one level up to an abstraction that sees it as an instantiation of a type.

Academia **29**

It's similar to the way we begin to compare religions only when we accept that there can be more than one—when we cease to take our own for granted; or comparative "literatures" when we still think that (say) the Germans or the French had different national "spirits" that informed their arts. But if we become uninterested in any specific religion at all, there is no point in comparing religions. Similarly, if we move on beyond the notion of national arts and literature—if it's all a polyglot hodge-podge, or all fragmentary memes, or all translated into English, or all unread—there are no longer substantial entities to compare. We will probably obsess about our neighbors if we live on a quiet tree-lined street and are home a lot, but in a Levittown where we come to only to sleep, we hardly consider them "neighbors" at all.

Or take another example. Philosophy too turned academic during the Modernist century, mutating from the situation-bound moralistic considerations of the Victorian age to a method of proceeding in its own right, more abstracted from individuals and more analytical. Even Kant and Hegel, the great systematizers, fit their structures into a world of individuals overseen by God, and in the case of Hegel a version of the Christian linear view of societies in history, the individual by nature part of a process of historic development reaching an apotheosis. A Hegel or a Marx did not think of themselves as "doing philosophy" but rather explaining the world. Now philosophy professors call themselves "philosophers"—the product their machines emit is something called "philosophy," the way a machine in Hershey, Pennsylvania spits out Hershey bars or chocolate kisses. The reaction against this (say in Bertrand Russell's rejection of Hegel's tripartite chains of ideas culminating in God Himself) put aside the Enlightenment building blocks of individuals, societies, and history in favor of abstract mathematical building blocks: it seems we don't need people at all! We can consider their products, words and actions.

Hegel showed his Romanticism by making statements purportedly true of all Germans, all French, all Westerners; Modernism said, Put that in scientific terms! Give me studies! But the process of Modernism from early to late has been one of gradual tessellation of generalities: we no longer speak of all Americans, or Germans, or "primitive" tribes—they have fractured into splinter groups defined by race, gender/sexuality, political persuasion, and so on. And this is where we can get social-scientific, expressing generalizations. The problem then becomes how to fit the individual back into the general rule. Crude sociology/anthropology/psychology/literary theory asserts that because a person/text/society is of a certain class/race/nationality, there follow certain things about that individual. And this isn't always correct, and in any case can't be assumed. To be sure, we've learned to some degree to resist these simplifications, and we are in the process of realizing that the very act of abstraction is itself suspect. At this point, we are ready to move on from Modernist "disciplines" and go back to particulars.

Modernism's emphasis on method rather than content meant that linguistic philosophy predominated, philosophy being made in words the way painting is an arrangement of shapes on a flat canvas. It became largely the analysis of how other terms mean, circling around Saussure's key notion (considered further below) that

30 What Hath Modernism Wrought?

words are signs that have meaning only by relation to other signs, rather than being something people produce in situations in the world that includes other people. And yet now, like the other academic humanities and social sciences, philosophy has separated itself from the world outside and become irrelevant to the lives of all but a few insiders, who continue to practice it for as long as the economics of higher education will allow.

Where do we go from here? The answer is: back to the individual. Not the unrepresentative exceptionally interesting genius of Romanticism, nor even to the gray "everyman" of anti-Aristotelean protagonists such as in Arthur Miller's *Death of a Salesman*. Rather, to the endlessly interesting and colorful life of the individual that each of us leads between birth and death. All of us have such lives, and each of us lives through this drama. For each of us, it seems new. Yet general considerations can help us understand it as we live it without reducing us to statistics or workings-out of a foreordained pattern. The result will not be an academic discipline, though it may well be carried out in classrooms by older people guiding the conversation of younger—and will not result in "knowledge" beyond that of the personal. These disciplines have had their day. Academia is due for a change, which is coming whether it is ready or not.

Yet the notion that Modernist academic departments of the humanities and social sciences make progress in adding to a store of knowledge—and so, are engaged (like scientists) in "research"—is so fundamental to their justification that no one inside the bubble is allowed to question this, or is ostracized if they do. But this notion is the result of the Modernism that birthed these as disciplines, with its sudden abstraction allowing even people and their products to look to that degree more like the inhuman and thus abstract entities that are the objects of study in the natural sciences, ranging in size from galaxies to blood corpuscles, all of them irrelevant to what I as an individual desire, think, or feel.

To diverge for a moment from the main stream of my argument, this abstraction of the knowledge of experts from what interests average people, namely their own desires and feelings, is the source of the alienation many of these people feel nowadays from anyone in a position of authority, intellectual or otherwise. Modernism split from the way most people see their lives, and this produced not only the increasing irrelevance of academia but the backlash of populist anti-intellectualism so evident in the West (perhaps especially America) of our day. This position of rejection of anything that comes from someone with an academic degree extends even to things that seem to experts purely scientific, such as epidemiology (which is intrinsically based on groups of people, not individuals) and the spread of diseases that the average person cannot see, such as viruses. People understand diseases like leprosy or smallpox or the black death because they see the effects on their own bodies or those of others. And I don't think anybody would deny the validity of a doctor showing them a cancer in an X-ray of their body—they can see that, after all. But a virus—that's too abstract for many people, especially one that they may or may not get. We should try to personalize these things as much as possible rather than talking in terms of probabilities and statistics that many people simply can't relate to.

The problem, as we can even see from this example, is not abstraction in itself. It's substituting abstractions about people for individual people, as Modernist academics tend to do. Scientists also deal in abstractions that transcend the particular, and this by definition. There is even pure science, as there is pure mathematics that never curves back to touch the world. But the abstractions of science are not people, but instead linguistically invented, and inhuman, entities. So there's no problem with considering these abstractly: they are made to be abstract, after all. They are intrinsically general with respect to the world, not specific. It's the application of this scientific paradigm to people that produces problems. And we see these problems in the general shambles of the Modernistic humanities and social sciences in universities at the end of the Modernist era.

Besides, none of this, aside from medicine, reaches outside the ivory tower. Indeed, it doesn't reach very far within it—not to the next department, and probably not even to the next office where the inhabitant does something completely different. It certainly isn't research, as is shown by the fact that it doesn't contribute to a common fund of knowledge. In fact, nobody cares. Nobody cares about your article in a scholarly journal nobody reads, one among hundreds if not thousands, that looks at an aspect of novel X or poem Y from the perspective of theorist Z. That handful of professors who are acolytes of theorist Z and are interested in novel X or poem Y read your article only to substitute their reading for yours. And then somebody offers yet another reading that modifies theirs.

Is this knowledge? Sure, of a sort. But knowledge ranges from the personal to the general, from the trivial to the important. Because something is knowledge, it isn't for that reason worth acquiring. We have to pick which knowledge to foreground based on things that matter. This is Weber's point with respect to the social sciences: we always choose what we focus on, and what we do with the results.[3] Objectivity in the humanities and social sciences is always the servant of the subjective. Individuals don't go away merely because they are found in the act of perceiving rather than in what is perceived. Modernism, which changed the focus of Romanticism from the individual to the abstract, has caused us to forget this.

There is, of course, a point to discussing in an academic setting what people do and produce. But literature (for example), or our discussion of it, has nothing to do with science. We should own this fact and base our actions upon it. This is what makes literature valuable, not worthless. It helps us understand life as lived, in all its unpredictability. Science envy is the primrose path the humanities and social sciences have gone down for over a century and that has ended in their chewing endlessly on their own irrelevance. We can back out of this dead end.

We need to re-humanize our conception of the world, which means we need to consider a point of view wider than that of Modernism and its home in institutions— or the bleeding outwards of their dogmas to the world, such as cancel culture of academics who have strayed from their domain. Outside will not necessarily be to the verdant nature of the Romantics that contrasted with the dreary black-on-white "research" of scholars (to echo *Faust*), nor to the star-gazing that Whitman recommended rather than attendance at the astronomer's lecture, but merely down a level of

32 What Hath Modernism Wrought?

abstraction to the everyday interactions of human beings. Why did she smile rather than speak? What did that tone of voice mean? When you read a book, ask: what questions is this work trying to answer? What are the qualities of the world the author has created? What effect does this word or phrase in a poem have on us? What aspects of the world does this analysis include, and what does it exclude?

Because all words come from our mouths or from under our fingers, they are intrinsically tied to the world around them, related to those who use them and those at whom they are directed, the way cutting a Valentine heart out of a piece of red construction paper leaves the negative—that can also be used as a card for Mom, as countless elementary or grammar school teachers have pointed out. Words come to be in the form they take as they exit human beings, as if our mouth or fingers were the tip of a tube of toothpaste where the tube is all our body. We are not subjective to their objective, or the objective of the world; all of these are stirred into the fact of speaking or writing, and these can only be separated at our peril. It's individuals who cause specific words to come to be, so we can't consider words at whatever level of complexity as if they were natural objects.

Modernism works at a level of abstraction far above the individual. This was once an exciting point of view to adopt, but now it has run out of important things to consider, and abstractions do not link to particulars, but only to other abstractions. I am most fundamentally interested in what a single person, any single person, says or writes, because in this act of saying or writing, all the elements of self, others, world, particular and general are united. If we start with the separated product, words or the work, by contrast, we can't put the toothpaste back in the tube, put back into the work the individual and the world of others that gives form to the utterance. The relationship with the world and with others is assumed to be one of alienation, as abstractions necessarily are to particulars. Instead, we can consider the relation of the individual to the world as being the nexus of connection, assuming fusion of the world rather than primordial separation into its abstracted elements that, like Humpty Dumpty, cannot be put together again. We can see the work as equivalent to the instant the toothpaste comes out of the tube that unites the cloud from which words emanate with the world, the moment of birth that both causes the work/words to come to be.

Having students read works in college with a professor has a point, even if this is only that the students wouldn't otherwise read these works at all, and works can help them understand themselves. But the current way of offering the specific literary work as if it were nothing but the instantiation, identical to all other individual instantiations, of a theoretical abstraction, is both useless to the students and lethal to their interest—and satisfies no one but the professor who insists on this abstraction. Of course, if somebody hands us *Pride and Prejudice* or *David Copperfield*, we are already dealing with a personal product that has been born, toothpaste outside the tube. We can't be inside the head of Austen or Dickens. But we can ask questions that acknowledge that this was made by a person, realize that the work unites the elements of the cloud and the world outside, rather than being separate from them.

The idea isn't to evoke the historical circumstances of the author, because the way we see these is not the way the author did. But we can ask what questions what we are reading seems to be asking and what answers it gives: how do these relate to our own questions? Our own situation? We are people reacting to something made by a person, not scientists. We can ask these questions: What is the effect of the author introducing Character X here and having her do Y? How does the author present A or B? How is this shown? What happens to them? Is it retribution or reward? Why (plausibly) does the poem begin with this? What is the effect on the reader—you, and/or any reader—of this or that, these words or that alteration of viewpoint? Are there patterns in the details that tell us what is important to the author? What is the effect on us of the author using words C or D? What issues is the author taking on? What is her point? What is the effect of the repeated insistence by Character E that F or G? So-called close reading, sure—but not for its own sake, rather with an eye to understanding how we can use this work to help us consider our own life, which is the context in which we read it. And it's possible that some—many?—works we read will have no relation to our lives; no problem, just move on. We don't owe works or their writers anything at all. Thus we notice things in what we read not as an end but as a means to help us understand the way the work was formed by the author, and (to the extent that we can) why, as a means to understanding how it can help us understand our own life.

Professors of literature, who lead discussions of individual works for groups of individual readers, have to be aware of individual variations at all levels: we can't assume either that the author or a reader or groups of readers is/are in sync with broadly held attitudes. The first question is always: what is the author saying here? Nor can we assume that the author includes X or Y because she actually likes X or Y. Apparently Shakespeare used his borrowed potboiler "bad leader" and "lovers with difficulties" plots as mere hooks to hang his poetry on: perhaps that's what he had to do to fill the Globe. We can't try to read the mind of the author—that's a useful Modernist corrective of the Romantic obsession with "genius." But by asking what the effect on various readers of the fact that A or B is in the work, we can characterize what it is with respect to various worlds or circumstances. The work radiates out in all directions: backwards into the given of the author and forwards into the worlds in which it is read.

So sure, we can read a novel or a poem in a group and talk about it. That has its points, so long as we remember that its purpose is to get students to try to see if this work helps them understand themselves and their world. What academic literary study is not is an independent discipline that adds to a store of knowledge. The notion that academic literary study forms a discipline and creates a body of knowledge, even one that furthers the ends of particular striver groups, has to be abandoned with the waning of the Modernism that created it. We can continue to have an English or French Department, if we see these just as the places where we do things with literature in these languages. They are places to think about things we don't usually think about when we are leading our lives elsewhere, going to the store or going on a run or cooking dinner or taking out the garbage. Professors of literature aren't people transmitting a body of knowledge, but rather people (we hope) adept at guiding conversations, keeping things more or less on track and throwing in new ideas when the conversation lags. Professors are the servants of their students, not—as Modernism imagined—their masters.

Notes

1 For example, *Sociology of Religions; The Religions of China; The Religions of India: Hinduism and Buddhism; Ancient Judaism.*
2 Said, *Orientalism.*
3 Weber, "The 'objectivity' of knowledge."

5

MUSEUMS

Change is coming for academia, and change is coming for the arts as well. The art of late Modernism—to the extent that it has not morphed into the social activism of even later Modernism that is even more involuted and exclusionary—now takes place, and takes its place, within the hall of mirrors of other works in the museum, and so loses its connection to the lives of the outsiders to this hall of mirrors. The arts, like academic humanities and social sciences, have spent the huge intellectual fortune of their inception—the glory days of Matisse, Picasso, Braque, and the post-Impressionists, to stay only in French painting—and now are reduced to nickel and dime transactions of no interest but to people so close to their own world they can't see how trivial they are. This echoes the way splinter groups nourished by the bubble mentality of late academic Modernism demand alterations to how people talk, or changes in names of buildings and institutions, much as late Modernist art is about demanding entrance into, and/or attacks upon the museum.

Footsore tourists go to museums of contemporary art, if at all, to visit the gift shop or marvel at what appears to them the inanity of it all (my dog could do that!). Of course, insiders dismiss these scoffers as Philistines who fail to understand the well-policed rules that make Art Object X or Y a brilliant commentary on previous artworks. You thought sculpture had to be rounded like people? Check out David Smith's arrangements of flat rectangles in glistening whirly-surfaced steel! And even more mechanistic than that, Donald Judd's empty steel boxes with baked-on industrial color! You thought painting had to blend colors with a brush? Check out paint thrown in loops (Jackson Pollock) or running pours (Morris Lewis) or paintings of boring things like the American flag where you are supposed to admire the brushstrokes (Jasper Johns) or canvases all one flat color, say black (Ad Reinhardt). You thought canvases were flat? We can go beyond that too—say by making slits (Lucio Fontana).

These examples (such as Pollock, Louis, the repetitive blotches of Clyfford Still, Mark Rothko's equally repetitive fuzzy floating rectangles) are all from mid-century,

DOI: 10.4324/9781003217688-6

36 What Hath Modernism Wrought?

now considered classics. Art has continued apace since then, with works that are merely commentary on other works and lack even the visual appeal of these mid-century classics. Many give up trying to be interesting as objects and settle for late Modernist intellectual gotchas. We don't compare art works to the world, but to other works. And it's true that only insiders have the ability to do this. But the fact that outsiders don't get the point doesn't show how stupid and uncultured outsiders are, but only how involuted insiders are.

Of course, the insiders are right: if you are versed in the methodology, these seem like giant steps, brilliant achievements. To outsiders they merely seem trivial. It's quite true that Modernist art, even early Modernist, is technique-poor and concept-heavy—and it decreases the importance of separable technique, and increases the importance of the concept, the longer the Modernist century wears on. So outsiders dismiss them as products of their dog or three-year-old. For insiders, the point is that your dog's work would never be in a museum, and Artist X's is, the point of reference now being the museum, not the world. This is the involution, and institutionalization, of Modernism.

And now the notion that whatever the artist says is art is in fact art—which means, is to be included in the museum—has generalized to the insistence that whatever anybody in a group that can gain traction says should be included in the museum should be included. It is this inclusion in the museum that, as always under late inward-looking Modernism, is the primary goal. Thus criteria of value or worth that exclude works by members of groups demanding inclusion are held to be there for the purpose of keeping them out. Even museums of traditional art are attacked as themselves failing to mirror the sensibilities of late Modernism. Works represent groups, no longer individual works.

The assumption behind such attacks is late Modernist: the museum itself is the standard of value. If I'm not in the museum, I am being silenced. No museum presence, no voice. This does not, as traditionalists have asserted, attack the museum. It glorifies the museum as the only place worth being. It's even more involuted than mid-century Modernism, which at least argued that its works did too have the artistic heft—albeit as alternatives to other artworks—to merit inclusion. (Early Modernism had simply gone about its business and allowed others to claim that, though technique-poor, it was major art: it itself was not focused on the museum.) But museums were originally founded on the assumption of value of their contents, not the assumption that the museum conveyed value on its contents—which is where we had arrived by mid-twentieth century. Now we have abandoned the idea of value of works (rather than of the museum) at all, much as the fact that a social media influencer has X many followers is the end of the story. Not X followers because s/he does whatever, just because s/he has the followers. It's what we call famous for being famous. Works don't make the museum; the museum makes the works. The museum is famous for being famous.

However, those eager to get works by members of their preferred group into museums are chasing a phantom. They assume that museums will always have the cachet they once did, whereas in fact it's these actions that are robbing even encyclopedic museums of meaning and clout. Now visual puns on classic works of Egyptian or Greek art by contemporary artists from what we define as non-white groups hang or stand in the same galleries as originals to show "inclusion." The connection is purely Modernist, a visual echo like the concatenation of Medieval with Modernist works so dear to Dr. Barnes in his Foundation. Or the echoes of shapes in the Pennsylvania Dutch ironwork that he insisted had to be nailed above them.

Putting (say) a large slashing depiction of anti-Black violence in the Museum of Modern Art near the "Demoiselles d'Avignon" (the same gallery where once Picasso's "Guernica" hung, now returned to Madrid) is a moderately amusing joke like the combinations of old and new pictures in the Barnes Foundation. It's there because of the color of the artist and the people portrayed as under attack in the painting, but for Modernism it's just another flat surface to which the social state-ment of its inclusion or content is irrelevant. The new looks like the old. That's because it's a conscious echo of the old. But we can't re-connect the abstractions of Modernist art to the world by changing the contents of the museum. Whatever they look like or whoever they are by, they are still just the contents of a museum, things hanging on a wall or sitting on a pedestal. Whatever is being taught in a classroom or whoever is teaching it, it's still a college course in a classroom. In both the cases of the museum and the college, the object is defined by its place in institutions that matter a great deal to insiders and far less to outsiders.

The joke with the museum is the same as the joke with college humanities and social sciences: the fight is over places on the stage for a dwindling audience and a room that will soon be empty, and not just because of Covid-19. Museums worked, for the period they did, as collections of $1 + 1 + 1 +1$, not as systematized teaching tools, as Dr. Barnes—influenced by the Modernist thinker John Dewey, whose unit of consideration was the abstraction of "art," not individual works—misconceived his collection.[1] The Barnes works were best appreciated out of their legally-ordained context in Merion Station in the exhibit in Paris at the Musée d'Orsay while the Merion Galleries were closed. Back in their same configuration in the re-creation of their galleries now located in central Philadelphia, they are in competition with too much clutter again, unless the viewer simply picks out favorites or major paintings and ignores the very thing Dr. Barnes wanted them to be aware of. Namely the fact that whether the right-angled canvases (one excep-tion to the right angles: the Matisse dancers in the main room) were painted in the fifteenth century or the twentieth, in China or France, they are still shapes and colors that echo other shapes and colors. That's how the Modernists saw the Afri-can pieces in the Barnes collection as well, as interesting new-to-Westerners ways to make sculpture. Not as including artists of color.

The twentieth- and now twenty-first-century museum altered as Modernism waned, losing power for outsiders at every step of the way but gaining it for insi-ders. Though museum visits increased before the Covid-19 pandemic in contrast to all other venues of classical arts (such as concerts), this was certainly due to the fact that they are prestige destinations in the centers of much-visited cities: all we can

38 What Hath Modernism Wrought?

trace is the number of people entering, not the length of their stay or degree and nature of involvement with the works. I have sat for long periods of time in galleries in Washington's National Gallery where people stream through whole collections of Rembrandt without so much as slowing down, or say things before moving on like "Is that a real Rembrandt?" The countless visitors who take selfies in front of the "Mona Lisa" in the Louvre (which they cannot in any case approach closely enough to actually look at it) are documenting their presence in the same room with this famous object rather than meditating on Leonardo's artistry. Museums with any sense have beefed up the gift shop and the cafeterias or snack bars. When the Barnes Foundation was in relatively inaccessible Merion and subject to the whims of Dr. Barnes's visitor restrictions, it didn't attract enough visitors to pay its upkeep. That's why it was moved to the center of downtown Philadelphia. Now it's a tourist attraction. The point isn't the works, it's checking the list of visitor must-sees. After the Barnes, the statue of Rocky. And then run up the steps!

Public museums were founded in the early nineteenth century as tools of education and improvement, exposing the bourgeoisie of the Industrial Age to the Culture to which only princes and the aristocracy had hitherto had access. The aim of improvement faded as the impossibility of this endeavor became clear, but the aura of the museum remained, with the institutions that conferred power and prestige on their contents becoming themselves the point, the standard to be achieved or rebelled against. Modernist art, jumping with both feet into abstraction and breaking with the micro-realism of nineteenth-century salon painting, was at first excluded, then included. It wasn't the Modernist artists who demanded their inclusion, but academics. And this was initially against strong opposition. The seminal question by others about Modernist art was: Is this worthy of a museum?

The Matisse-heavy collection of Gertrude Stein's friends Etta and Claribel Cone was left to the Baltimore Museum of Art at the death of the longer-lived sister Etta in 1949 on the condition that "the spirit of appreciation for modern art in Baltimore became improved." By mid-century it had apparently done so, as the Museum accepted this astonishing collection, now the BMA's calling card. These days, by contrast, at the end of Modernism, the museum is no longer external to art; instead art is intrinsically in dialogue with the museum, which has become the most important factor in the definition and indeed production of art. What does it mean for X or Y to be inside the museum? What does it mean to be outside? What counts as art? What, that is, is the transformation wrought on the everyday by its passage into these halls and positioning on a stand with an artist's name on a tag in front of it? In 2020, the Baltimore Museum tried (unsuccessfully, as it turned out—the resistance was too great) to sell works by white males to buy more works by women and artists "of color." They didn't try to sell the Matisses.

Modernism is a viewpoint created by insiders, with its interests insiders' interests. Yet this view has been foisted on us all, much as the artist-focused Modernist view of art that made the givens of the work its subject matter came to define the age. It was a view of a certain sub-group that was unduly generalized, and now whose specificity has begun to be clearer as academia and its proponents have begun to

Museums   **39**

recede in power and prestige. Here, I am echoing Nietzsche's point, and Weber's too (as well as Foucault's), that certain groups find certain ideas more congenial than they find other ideas, or than other groups do. Islam, for example, was in Weber's view a warriors' religion, Buddhism at least initially a religion of individuals who had withdrawn from normal life, and Judaism the dogged adherence to laws to insist upon God's partiality toward a pariah group.[2] Modernism served academics and museum curators, not other people.

Museums in late Modernism are as if on split screens: what they mean to insiders (if they don't let my work in, they are being racist/sexist) and what they mean to outsiders (everybody talks about it, and they're here and air-conditioned, and they're on the list of Top Attractions in City X). A similar development and turning inward characterizes the academic humanities and social sciences. This matters to insiders—if it's not on the syllabus, my group is being excluded; if someone of my persuasion is not a tenured professor, we are being dissed—but not to outsiders. Gotta pass this course to get my Hum/SS requirement!—to the extent that such requirements still exist.

Splinter groups demand guaranteed inclusion into these institutions, or change of naming rights on buildings—no other changes of the world required. It's these same people who demand that statues in public squares come down—the square is the same whatever the statue, even no statue, might be—though empty plinths don't make much visual sense. And the more central the square, the more vociferous the demands. But the changes sought are symbolic: nobody demands that the University of Virginia, for example, be destroyed because it was founded by a slave-owner and used slaves in its construction—only that it have a monument to the slaves who helped build it. And maybe cease mentioning Thomas Jefferson. If it's so tainted, why be part of it at all? Why not destroy it? But that's not the point. The point isn't to change the world, it's to keep the same world but give the splinter groups a bigger share of it. So now we have the monument in Charlottesville, an attractive circle that most people will use to sit. Demanding the excision of Jefferson from his university isn't trivial enough for late Modernism, and is a bridge too far—as those demanding it already knew. So that isn't happening.

It's the triviality of late Modernist focus on institutions rather than on the world outside, whether in theoretical articles or street protests, that makes clear how little energy it has left. Few people aside from those demanding these changes care about the skin color of those who made the objects in museums, or the sexual or racial group that the teacher of a college course belongs to. For students, it's about the degree and secondarily the course content, not staffing issues, any more than visitors to museums care about keeping track of works by members of groups X and Y. Besides, visitors to museums don't have to look at anything they don't want to. Nor do they have to take most college courses. Or look at the name of the building as they hurry into it, late for class or an appointment.

Modernism, with its focus on abstraction, has privileged the abstraction itself rather than, now, in late Modernism, remembering that abstraction hooks to the world—or becomes its own end and separates from the world, as it has done in

40 What Hath Modernism Wrought?

academia and the rarified world of contemporary arts. Abstraction has a purpose, but it is not intrinsically valuable. The death of Modernism is written into its failure to remember that it separated from the world for a reason, and in thinking that the separation itself was the goal. It's usual for movements to forget their origins after a while, after all, simply because of the passage of time: that was all so long ago!

Early Modernism didn't have this problem, as it was all about justifying the separation: of course it knew the world was there. And this forgetting is not all negative. Teenagers don't rebel against their parents unless they are extremely aware of the parents. But if their whole lives are defined by their parents, they have failed to achieve independence and to live their own lives. Modernism and its offspring are all defined by this initial peeling away from the world: as it got further in time from the peeling, this lost its strength. Now few people even remember this Promethean act. And Modernism has failed to define itself in any other way. We are running on the last ripples of energy of an act that has long since subsided into senescence.

Modernism took for granted that people were interested in art and would put up with—no, welcome—its rigors and *longueurs*. Consider the fictional Gustave von Aschenbach of Thomas Mann's *Death in Venice*, a world-famous writer according to the novella, whose death is received, at its end, by a "respectfully shocked world." Art still mattered to the Modernists—perhaps more than anything else. After all, according to Matthew Arnold, some decades earlier, art is what replaced religion—although problematically.[3] Modernism took the artwork and hence the museum for granted—assuming that people were interested in what was in museums—and thus focused on the work. For Postmodernism, the museum itself is the point—what's in it, what isn't. Or for larger artworks, what's art, what isn't. And few people care as much about the museum, or about what art is or isn't, as artists.

Postmodernism is insider art because it's ruminations about the process and nature of what artists do. It's theoretical, abstract like all of Modernism. The idea of having the Hirshhorn Museum in Washington, DC show the plans and legal documentation that made Christo's "Running Fence" possible, for example, is more interesting than either the deadeningly legalistic documentation itself (oh, they say, that's the point! To show you how boring this stuff is! But I don't need to go to a museum to experience boredom), or the intrusive expensive structure of the fence itself, fencing nothing out and nothing in and ending in the ocean, that it documents. Let's make a house that nobody lives in and have tourists admire it—full, say, of 1950s suburban tackies! Let's take machine parts and hang them in art galleries! Let's make artworks that are put where nobody sees them but that artists are still supposed to be credited with! Oh. All done already.

Because Postmodernism started with the Modernist focus on the artwork as a given rather than something to be achieved, it produced art about art. Those lacking a background in the history of this transformation tend to find the result either incomprehensible or whimsical, but rarely profound. Is a huge clothespin in a city plaza even comprehensible any more given that few people in cities, or indeed anywhere else, use clotheslines? Is the fact relevant, that with its two "legs" and a round top, it sort of looks human? Why is it so Lenin-statue-large? The factory parts in museums have interesting shapes, sure, but interesting enough to justify taking up all this room? Can't we see something similar in a real factory?

Or hmmm. This one looks like a Campbell's Soup can (or rather, two) but it's made of bronze and the label is painted on and it's inside a museum in a glass case. I may have Campbell's Soup cans in my pantry. So why visit the museum to look at this? OK, let's give it a try. It's expensive materials, and it took work by people to create something like what machines stamp out in an instant. What's up with that? A commentary on mass production and its inhumanity? Class, discuss! And here we have a room that could have come from Vienna ca. 1890 complete with potted palms and piped-in waltzes. Is it art to re-create the clichés of the past? Is a large plaster block representing the interior of a very small room art? It turns the void solid—what are the implications of this? Why not the interior of an airplane hangar? Too big for a museum! I get it, I get it! It's all about the museum. But actually, it's pretty trivial. However, I can't say this or I'll flunk the class. This will all be on the test.

The purpose of explaining the first generation of Modernist art was to get us to appreciate its complexity. With Postmodern art and after, there is no complexity—we can get it in an instant, perhaps by ourselves or more likely, when someone tells us what the point is. Early Modernism usually required professors, but it ultimately returns us to the world because that's what it's about. Postmodernism also relies on professors, only it doesn't return us to the world. The result is that tourists see museums of contemporary art as air-conditioned silliness with snack bars and gift shops, and the (always grayer) audience at classical music events dreads the occasional piece of contemporary music at the beginning.

Museums and academia, the home grounds of Modernism and its descendants, have become largely irrelevant to the world outside them. The academic disciplines of the humanities and social sciences that came into existence and flourished in the twentieth century and have limped into the twenty-first are doomed to extinction, or radical re-conceiving. What they cannot do is continue forever in their current exhausted state.

Notes

1 Dewey, *Art as Experience.*
2 Weber, "The Religions of Civilization and Their Attitude to the World."
3 Matthew Arnold, "The Study of Poetry."

PART II
Abstraction

6

EXPLANATION

The default and base position of life is no words at all. We just are. When the tapestry of life comes smoothly off our loom, we focus on what we are doing in the moment. We can analyze where we are, but only for a reason. All boats float on the surface of the water, no matter how deep. We can measure the depth, but we don't have to do this, as we are always on the surface.

Analysis comes when threads in the warp and woof of life ball up, or the shuttle gets stuck or falls off, or things don't lie flat. This means we only ask for explanation of the things that need explanation: if things are normal, we typically don't. It's usually only when we expect the dog to bark and it doesn't, or the reverse, that we sense something amiss. It's when somebody gets sick that we go to the doctor—or we go to the doctor pre-emptively to make sure we stay well. After all, if we lived forever in perfect health, we would never go to doctors. If we can walk perfectly well, we don't go to physical therapy for walking. If we read well, we don't go to a reading specialist. Even general questions have specific starting points: it's when we suddenly doubt our senses, as Descartes did by looking out the window and seeing a man in a big hat below (or was it?), that we wonder if we are getting correct information at all, ever.

Responding routinely to a catch or tear in the warp and woof of our lives presupposes that we have already (so to say) gotten out of the particularity of experience enough to have a notion of what can go wrong. If I can walk, I walk. If I am hearing, I hear. Only if there is a difficulty do we say, there is a snag: I can't walk, or hear. If a doctor (say) can fix this, it's only because somebody has gotten out of the level of noting snags to understand how hearing in general, or walking in general, works. At its most general, that's what we call science, but we do this all the time at a more personal level, where we are our own doctor based on experience. And sometimes we can't immediately diagnose the problem, any more than doctors can.

46 Abstraction

Why did this branch fall? Oh (looking up): it was dead and we obviously had a wind storm—look at all the other smaller branches and leaves that are down! Why isn't the milk where I left it? Oh, one of the kids. Or an intruder in the house? Or the whole shelf in the fridge fell down? Or more general: why does this side of the lawn grow better than the other? Perhaps an experiment, testing hours of sunlight for each? We can simply check every (say) half hour over (say) a month (is this enough?). Or we can set a photometer? Our thesis is that this difference is due to sunlight difference—let's say we find this difference. Is the effect more or less than we expect? What if it's the expected amount—does this mean that it was the sunlight? Or is this a case of correlation being mistaken for causality? I have two sons. I am finding evidence of food eaten in the basement where we have occasionally had mice, and therefore where we tell the boys not to eat. The older boy goes to college. The signs of eating continue. Is this proof that it's the younger? A strong suggestion? Who else could it be? We have eliminated one variable and now have new data.

This applies "scientific methods," but because it seems too limited in interest (nobody cares about my lawn but me, or my basement), it does not qualify as what most people would call science. People getting too intensely scientific on things that we think affect only them or trying to re-invent the wheel (everybody knows grass needs sunlight) fall into the category of cranks, those who produce unreadable books like Casaubon in George Eliot's *Middlemarch*, or the strange private artworks of obsessed people that we call Visionary Art and that we can spend a few minutes with, admiring their strangeness. Science isn't a specific undertaking, it's the same undertaking as figuring out where we left our keys or why the milk isn't where we left it, only on issues that matter to many people and that are important to them. And the issues we can get funding for. Science is not merely personal; it's socially defined—which makes sense given that it's about extra-personal entities. Extra-personal to too few people? Not interesting. Perhaps still science, for the few people, but it's not individuals who define science. It's the collective.

We start this process at whatever level by asking for explanation of something. But even this is determined by circumstances. Whether or not we ask for explanations is up to us: that isn't something that logic or science or philosophy can adjudicate, because it's the demand for explanation that lies behind all of these. Some people never seek to understand why even something very negative and very unexpected has happened: we call these people "fatalistic," not asking for explanations. So if we follow a whim (?) or are of a certain personality (?—insert particular individual-based phrase here meaning we can't say, like the preference for chocolate over vanilla, or liking Mozart), we can be curious and ask for explanations. Usually we wait for snags, but some people don't wait for something to go bad before they look into how the world works.

Still, we can ask why for anything, but only if we can conceive of an alternative. For example, why do people get old and wear out? At one point we'd have said, that's just the way it is, or it's God's plan. Now perhaps we add what we know about telomere length. Why do people have five fingers? We have to compare it to an alternative for this to be a question. What we say and do is formed by the world under specific circumstances.

Explanations are abstract; that's how they function. When we ask for explanation, we shift to another gear. But that doesn't mean that all abstractions are explanation. We can have abstractions that don't clearly hook to the world at all. These can be, say, mathematical. Pure mathematics don't threaten anyone. Neither does science, short of blowing us up, because it is made of entities that are not human. What threatens us as humans are abstractions of humans that are substituted for the particularities of people. These are purely academic, except when they become political, at levels that vary from large to small. Individuals don't matter, only their economic position in a Darwinian world of conflict—so *Viva la Revolución*! Or: take my college class because I show you that texts relate only to other texts, words to other words, and by the way, if you say something different on the final, you won't pass the class.

This is not the humanist insistence that people come first, or the position of the mind over brain people (see below). It's not a content objection on my part to say that people are scooped up by abstractions that refer to racial groups or economic classes. That makes it seem as if we have two fighting on the same field, whether groups or classes. The point is rather that abstractions are not particulars. Nobody denies that I am a particular compared to you. Those who defend considering the abstraction and not the particular have to argue that what these people have in common that produces the abstract is more important than what makes them particular—for example, Freud's patterns for all people, or males, or females, or Marx's insistence that everyone in an economic class can be considered as if identical.

But here's where Hume's point in his *Enquiry Concerning Human Understanding* kicks in—the point that even Hume himself apparently misunderstood. Namely that we can't justify an abstraction by amalgamating particulars. He's quite right about that: we can't say whether the sun will rise tomorrow merely because it has done so every other day. But we can say that as long as the planets stay in their orbits, it will. And that should have been Kant's response: explanations are abstractions that decouple from particulars and so can contextualize variations between them (say, the sun not rising). If we see or imagine a variation at the level of particulars, such as the sun not rising, we cannot explain this variation at the level of particulars. If one flower is red and another is yellow, we can't explain this (assuming we ask for explanation) by noting the difference. We have to move to a more abstract level—species of flowers, say, or chemical compounds. But we don't get there by adding particulars.

This is not an argument about the relative importance of individual human variations, and doesn't require postulates of a soul or a mind. If we are at the level of individuals, we consider individuals—and nobody says it's impossible to consider individual people. Nor can we say that it's illegitimate to leave that level for more abstract ones—we do it all the time on an informal basis: all women X or Y, or all men (we don't have to be right, and we have to learn the dangers of generalizing on too little evidence), or almost all teenagers or baristas or basketball players or

48 Abstraction

suburban dads or whatevers as a group. But we have to have a reason for considering these as groups, and all such generalizations that amalgamate individual people into types about which we say A or B are like Hume's 1 + 1 + 1 generalizations that by definition never add up to science. If we want science, we have to kick into another gear, one of abstraction from individuals. That's the level of corpuscles and body structure, not the level of (say) racism or benevolence.

The level of racism and benevolence is the extremely fertile field of the social "sciences," which of course aren't sciences at all, but Humean well- or less well-justified amalgamations of individuals. My point is not that this isn't knowledge, because of course it can be, just the way it's knowledge about my cat that when he doesn't come down in the morning to be brushed, he's probably sick, or that if a woman doesn't laugh at my jokes when I am trying to please and come on to her, we're not going to end up in bed. Or that young men are hot-headed and have to be handled in a certain way. But it's a field that always flirts with the danger of trying to turn Hume into Kant, to claim that correlations in perceived qualities implies causality and hence identity in the group that's considered as a group.

The siren song that leads Modernist humanities and social sciences astray is the song of science, the rocks it founders on the promises of the alchemy of turning correlation into causality. We can't actually ever do that, any more than other metals could actually be turned to gold. But it's a song academic disciplines seem unable to resist, because those quasi-scientific claims make headlines and less absolute generalizations don't, and if they're general knowledge rather than folksy cracker-barrel-style generalizations, they seem to justify a place in universities. The social sciences so-called aren't disciplines, they are an amorphous place on a scale with personal views at one end and science at the other. Under the pressure to seem academic, things in this middle area as they developed in the Modernist century are always getting too close to the edge of claiming they are science. They need to accept that they aren't, but that this isn't a bad place to be at all, for the same reason that reading novels rather than doing plasma physics isn't a waste of time: we're all individuals, and seeing other individuals as the unit of choice is perfectly legitimate.

The edge of the social sciences closest to science is the most exhilarating, but also the most dangerous: Marx or Freud, or early anthropology, or the theory of racial types. Here is where the biggest claims emerge about people: finally we understand us! These colossal claims (gender/class/economics/race) seem to simplify a lot of things. Only they always over-reach by failing to consider differences among individuals grouped together under these vast rubrics. They are still trying to wring Kant out of Hume.

A hair further on the scale into the closest edge of the realm of science is a position even more fraught with danger, because it is real science held to explain individual actions: claims for evolutionary biology that explain our actions, determinism by DNA, or the "gay gene." Of course, the scientific part here can be valid, because it's abstract. What's problematic is trying to apply this abstraction to another level entirely, the level of individuals. We can talk about genes or heritability of red hair, but this doesn't explain individuals *if we consider them as individuals*. The argument is not that my individuality is more important than what I have in common with others in particular groups to which I belong. In fact, we might say that my individuality is produced precisely by the amalgamation of all my group memberships, like defining me as the space in the middle where countless circles in a Venn diagram overlap.

This is a more sophisticated argument than we generally hear nowadays. Now we are surrounded by claims for social science causality that are as ham-fisted as Marx's insistence that (say) all rich people or all factory workers are interchangeable—what the more nuanced Weber rejected by pointing out that no amount of history of social or economic classes can explain Raphael's production of the *Sistine Madonna*. [1] Nowadays these claims tend to take the form of racial generalizations—usually by the very people who deny the validity of grouping people into races (a denial that is quite legitimate if it gets too close to making claims to science). "Speaking as a LatinX, gay man, Boricuan, Dominican, Black lesbian, etc., I…" An individual is logically indistinguishable from the group. This sort of claim is the logical end of Modernism that used science as the magnet to pull the academic social sciences and humanities out of the realm of personal observations and into their self-understanding as disciplines that contribute to a store of knowledge.

The relationship between abstract and particular is always up for negotiation, whether in everyday use or as the basis for science in laboratories—and these are all parts of the same scale with no clear line between them. We label events in the world based on our knowledge level and our desires, which can change. Something that could maybe work is worth a try. We want X to happen and take steps that we know may achieve it, but don't get it. Bad luck. What if we are pretty sure Y will cause X but it doesn't? Hmm. What did we do wrong? Maybe we just need to do it again? That's how we operate, whether we are trying to find our keys, or split the atom.

Thus the conclusions of science, when viewed in the rear-view mirror, frequently seem ridiculously wrong: hindsight is 20/20, but not reality. But that isn't a problem; science is always about being wrong because it's about individual people working at a non-individual level. You feel the need to do this because of individual factors, but actually doing it is a leap into the dark onto a whole new level. You can't get to the abstract from amalgamating individuals (Hume again). For example, take Victorian medicine, which drives a lot of people crazy nowadays. How could all these self-important men with beards have insisted on senseless interventions for, for example, pregnancy and childbirth—involving women, whose bodies were imperfectly understood or misunderstood, when in fact none of the treatments did a bit of good and most were harmful? (They got people to listen to them: misplaced respect for authority, we would say.) Or the centuries before that where doctors bled patients to let out "humors" and made patients ingest substances we now know to be neutral at best and poisonous at worst? The patients failed to get better, or died, sometimes tortured to death by the doctors' actions. Why didn't they draw some conclusions? we ask angrily. But they did, just

50 Abstraction

not our conclusions. The patient dying (perhaps) only showed how tenacious this illness was that it defeated even the experts!

Now we shake our heads, or rail about the patriarchy. But the fact that sacrificing to the weather gods didn't always produce good weather didn't mean the gods weren't there. Maybe the sacrifices were wrong or insufficient or tainted? Or the gods simply otherwise engaged or on somebody else's side? The Greeks never knew if a specific god/goddess was helping them in battle or the reverse—and even propitiating the right one wasn't a guarantee of a positive outcome for you if s/he was already committed, as Athena was to the Greeks at Troy or Aphrodite/ Venus was to the Trojans. None of this was illogical, and we can even call the postulations of causality a form of science if we like.

Demanding that science always be at the level we have subsequently obtained is like thinking away the time it took to figure out where we left the keys. We only kick into science mode when we need to know something, or are in the dark. The history of science will always show more dark than light. Science is a process; we can't castigate the fact that it wasn't instantaneous.

Even religion, belief just because, is intertwined with science, because both are way of understanding the world. Take the fact that treatments for illness can be anywhere on a scale of probability, from what we think of as certain, to improbable. What happens when we cross the line on the spectrum of probability from "all but certain" (say, prescribing steroids against poison ivy) to 50–50 (dunno but let's try) and then on to "we're out of ammunition"? This is where, at the extreme end of "certain nothing will work and the patient will die," and the patient gets better, some people speak of miracles. So of course miracles are possible: they aren't an absolute contrast to science, but part of the same scale. Miracles are the label we put on a specific situation: a desired outcome we believed to be close to 100% unachievable. But this is a fact of what we know and what we believe, and of our desire, as an unexpected turn for the worse is never called a miracle, only a turn for what we define as better. If we don't know whether what we can do will work, to return to the middle of the scale, and it does, that's not a miracle. Miracles are a situation under specific conditions of our knowledge. They are facts about us as much as they are about the world. People are always who and what they are with respect to the world.

Of course, we can speak of a miracle even if we ourselves do nothing. Unexpected good things are "miracles," just the way for some people unexpected bad things (premature death, fatal accidents) are "tragedies." Some groups issue further rules for calling something a "miracle." For the Catholic Church, someone has to have prayed to only one saint or would-be saint for the unexpected good thing to be certified as a miracle for that former person. Lesser degrees of improbability are merely seen as positive responses: the grottoes of countless statues of the Virgin in European churches are covered with plaques of gratitude for success on exams on specific dates. Or cures: that's why Latin America produces its ex voto images of limbs or heads to offer holy images. Presumably most of these were not miracles, and the student actually studied, or the arm got better.

I am not mounting an attack on working in the middle area between science and the personal. I am offering a warning about pushing such work toward science, as well as casting a skeptical eye on the structures of disciplines and "research" that have grown up in institutions under Modernism. There is nothing wrong with seeing and considering generalizations about people and their lives; indeed, it can be useful in understanding issues with individuals—and typically that's why we engage in them. For example: the middle class in country A or B nowadays does X or Y, the expectations for women in the Victorian era were largely Z, a house in postal code whatever in 2020 was likely to be a certain number of square feet/metres. The problem comes when instead of using the general to illuminate the particular, we use it to replace the particular. Not everyone in postal code whatever has a house of that number of square feet/metres. Not all Victorian women were Z. And beware of telling me what I believe merely because you know I am a straight white male.

The connection of Modernist abstractions to such notoriously unpredictable creatures as people (unpredictable by definition: because individuals—not because of human "free will") is therefore fraught with difficulties. If you treat people and their products in a scientific manner, you have to leave out the whole world of their particulars: specific uses of words, responses, questions, grunts, shrugs, inter-actions, parts or wholes of works of art that strike us as funny or profound, human relations we are happy about or stew over—all the minutiae of life that constitutes the day, not merely filling scientific rubrics but being the very stuff of life. The arts become effete and cold, and the human sciences always flirt with becoming versions of Marxism, using abstractions to render the individual irrelevant: it's this or that social structure that makes people do what they do.

Or it's evolutionary determinism: we do what we do because cave men did it and passed on the genes. But cavemen didn't write essays, and on computers; where did that come from? And they certainly didn't write this particular essay. That remains to be explained. We have to choose our connection with the past from abstractions that we can share with cave men (or whomever). That means genetic determinism works backwards. It's not predictive: it picks the current behavior it wishes to justify—say altruism or selfishness, preference for warm roofed-in places to sleep, or gender attitudes—and then finds a caveman or genetic equivalent. See? We're just like them! But obviously they weren't me living in my house, so what justifies our letting those facts be overlooked? Our choice of abstractions, nothing more. Abstractions of thought are not machines, they are just abstractions by individual particulars. The problem is what happens when we train our view only on the general and not the particular. We don't live in the abstract. We live in the particular. And if we forget that we have adopted an inhuman perspective on people and confuse the lens with the thing seen through it, we get the world wrong. That's problematic because we leave out things that matter to most people.

Weber's emphasis on the scientific aspect of the social sciences runs parallel to and is contemporaneous with the birth of Saussurian emphasis on *langue* rather than

52 Abstraction

parole (see below) and the Modernist focus on the apparently objective work: it's a wave that swept over the intellectual world: everybody running after the bitch-goddess (to use the term of William James) of success—which here means: of science. Weber was well aware of the positivist insistence that "is" couldn't imply "should" in the social sciences, but he was equally aware of my point that everything on the spectrum was related to everything else, and had varying admixtures of each of these. Weber remains appealing because (unlike the positivists) he was aware that the scientific aspect didn't replace or render useless the personal: the purpose of all academic objectivity by the professor was to let students make up their own (individual) minds.[2] In addition, the soulless drudgery of bureaucrats (including academic bureaucrats) that he thought characterized the modern age didn't itself prohibit change, it just worked the aftershocks of the explosions by charismatic leaders in thought.

Notes

1 Weber, "The 'Objectivity' of Knowledge," 373.
2 Weber, "The Scholar's Work."

7

SCIENCE ENVY

Modernism was the high water mark of academia, which is now behind us. With abstraction, everything is difficult, because we are no longer in the realm of the lived, something everybody has access to. It's outside of us, so we need professors to explain to us this mystifying state of being human. So much for the Enlightenment's notion that humans are the measure of all things. Now the measure of all things consists of their products and patterns, analyzed in isolation from the living, breathing, sweating human animals that they refer to, or who actually made them.

Given that the (quasi-)scientific view is so frigid and removed from what we do, the question arises immediately: How can we have been enamored of this cold apersonal view of things for so long? There is an answer to this: We weren't, but professors were, because this view served their view of themselves as being scientists—the gold standard of the Modern age. But science is a particular undertaking with particular qualities, as well as particular advantages and disadvantages. It's not universally applicable. Science becomes possible when we postulate a point of view that is at the opposite end of the spectrum from that of the individual human. The personal is always our underlying point of view, given that we are always individual humans. But it need not always be the content of this point of view, any more than we need always focus on the window rather than on what we see through it. We can sit in the US and talk about Rwanda, Australia, or Malta; we can be on Earth and talk about the universe; we can think about what we will be doing and who we will be 20 years from now.

The fact that for science the individual human is not the focus, is in fact meaningless as an individual, is the reason various Christian denominations and their moral expression—which are all about the individual and his place in the universe—had such strong negative views regarding the scientific POV from the Renaissance onwards. In the meantime, most of us have gotten used to science, but conflicts between one end of the spectrum and the other still occur. Science can

DOI: 10.4324/9781003217688-9

54 Abstraction

tell us how to have safer sex, but if a church and its attendant morality think we shouldn't be having any sex at all, or (say) none outside marriage, morality will object. *Pace* the logical positivists, who were expressing the then-new Modernist mentality by seeing science not only as the gold standard for undertakings but the only standard, not being scientific doesn't mean illegitimate or meaningless, it just means what people are doing is at another place on the scale.

Science is not the gold standard for all activities, and we should beware of its lure on individuals, because we can't get there (abstraction) from here (individuals), and the attempt to achieve this leads us off a cliff. (This is the basis of Karl Popper's noting, with Hume, that we can't justify an abstraction by amalgamating specifics—we don't get to deduction through induction: science starts with the abstraction and then sets out to see if it holds.[1]) The abstractions of science, despite the fact that they describe an objective world outside people, are not always appropriate. Science is abstract, but it's an abstraction that is evoked by particular individuals under particular circumstances. We can sometimes say scientific things about people, just as we can talk about speed and acceleration in reviewing the tapes of an auto accident where someone cut into traffic too fast. But we don't usually need to have recourse to this level of abstraction at all, nor is it always possible. If there is not yet (or ever) a video, perhaps because the event is in the process of happening and we don't yet know whether it will be an accident and hence of interest not just to us but to insurance companies, we just have to act. To see everyday life, such as entering traffic, from a scientific viewpoint, therefore, we need both a reason and an opportunity, and it is rare when both come at once. We have to see the world not in the present tense but in the past, here through video tapes: repeatable, not in the moment, off the firing line.

That's science, and the conditions of the laboratory. What's relevant when I merge into traffic is not science but me, the accelerator, my car, and what other cars are doing. We don't just get scientific on the world for no reason. Besides, science isn't a single pond we fish in: we have to find the right pond. How do I know that the applicable science here would be physics and not cell biology or astronomy? That's something we learn, not something evident from the experience. We intuit our way to scientific explanation, at least for new explanations of new problems (sixth grade science fair projects are already explained, as are many other things). We're like the reverse of the Prince in Cinderella: he had one shoe and was looking for the woman it fit, whereas scientists keep trying on multiple shoes until they find the one that fits the data they have.

Science is something people do even though it transcends them, not a list of terms, which in any case didn't always exist and had to be developed. Still, we say we "discovered" what was there all along and that the process of discovery is irrelevant to this fact, just as blood contained corpuscles before Leeuwenhoek saw them, and galaxies revolved before the Hubble telescope. But we humans had to want to discover them, or to figure out what they were if we stumbled over them. The individual works in a relationship with the world in science too, as well as (say) with words when I ask for, and get or don't get, a muffin; probably at any rate I don't get a rubber tire when I ask for a muffin unless I'm trying to speak a language I don't actually know or am bad at, or someone is playing a trick.

Sometimes, we can use the abstract to predict the future of the real. Given speed and gravity and acceleration (and so on), we should be able to get this rocket into orbit. And it works! Big victory for math and physics! Yet, once again, this is the same sort of reasoning as when we lose something in everyday life, say a credit card, and then go over our memories of what we did with it. We realize it has to be in the pocket of the coat we wore yesterday, remember the coat, and find it in the pocket! Thought leads us back to actuality. People did this long before the scientific revolution, even though this is the way scientific reasoning works too. Sometimes thought doesn't produce the results we wanted. We think about where the credit card should be, or may be, and look there. But the credit card isn't in that spot. Hmmm. Or the rocket, sadly, falls over, or blows up. It should have worked! That pesky reality. Guess there was something we didn't think of or didn't know about. Or did we just make a mistake in calculation?

We are always careening back and forth between abstract and particular, even in science—which makes sense, as science is a particular rabbit hole off our life of particulars: it attaches to particulars at a specific point—or fails to do so. A drug may have 100% effectiveness in the laboratory and impressive results in trials; nonetheless, it didn't work with Patient X. Perhaps this person had another condition we don't know about? We forgot to note that the trials were (say) only on males or Asians, and the patient is neither? Well, she isn't the same person as those in the trials either, but that isn't supposed to matter. Or does it here? Or let's say it generally works, only not with all. We don't know which group we belong to until we try it.

The techniques of science have to be developed. The notion of "double-blind" studies where it's not just the patient who doesn't know whether s/he is getting the experimental medicine or the placebo but also the doctor (so the doctor doesn't betray by body language which it is, or tilt the results to what s/he thinks likely or wants) was not the way science started out. Before people developed the notion of germs, and ways to minimize or eliminate them that actually cut down on fatalities, doctors didn't sterilize instruments—or even wash their hands. Science didn't spring fully formed from the head of Galileo or Newton. We're refining the steps of what we call the scientific process all the time. It changes, as the result of thought. Science doesn't justify this thought, it presupposes it: science is part of the same human spectrum as everything else.

Science abstracts from alteration and individuality to make statements that escape change and particular circumstances. It's uninterested in and indeed can't touch situations that are used up in the instant, or that are personal, such as whether I like painting X or beer Y; to get anything scientific out of this we have to abandon particularity and deal in other more abstract concepts entirely. Say: Do I enter traffic here or here? If it's seen as just this single situation, no science is possible. For this one case to have a relation to science we have to use or invent concepts that are universal and stay still long enough to be tested, things like force and weight

56 Abstraction

and velocity. These can in turn be applied to specific situations—but we don't need a scientific explanation of force and velocity to know when to enter traffic, any more than we need science to say whether we prefer painting X or Y.

Science both expresses and creates an inhuman world—but (here's the paradox) it's something people invented and do. This is no more bizarre than me saying "The world outside of me exists." Or "My native language is English but I speak French." Whether the statement is about corpuscles or galaxies, the individual human is irrelevant to science and all the vocabulary of people interacting with people: wishes, goals, hopes, morals, and so on. And that means my personal response to the assertion is irrelevant because it transcends the human. (I consider this fact more below.) Blood corpuscles may be inside our bodies, but they are not any more human than galaxies. They can change, but I can't change them; only impersonal forces or events can change them. Of course, I can help bring into effect the impersonal forces, much as I can decide to exercise for health, or to jump off a cliff to commit suicide. I can cause my own lung cancer by smoking, for example. I am not assuming there is an "I," just that that's one thing that can be said: listen! I (or "I") am saying it! If we decide that the "I" is a fiction, nobody keels over dead.

Science is abstracted from the world of humans who engage in it. But science can change the human world as it is bent back to the particular. Science is the search for the reproducibly true, which means abstracted from the messiness of life, and it is pursued under the purified and controllable conditions of the laboratory. But science doesn't have to end in the laboratory. It's useful, sometimes essential, in getting outside the lived to fix problems or expand horizons: illnesses can be addressed if we label them as more than individual cases and discover how to cure them, rockets can be sent into space if we think in terms of gravity and thrust, earthquakes and storms can be predicted if we work on a more abstract level than whether the bullet in Watson's leg in the Sherlock Holmes stories (sometimes shoulder; Conan Doyle evidently forgot sometimes) predicts rain.

It seems likely that the amazing results for science in the Victorian age and early twentieth century made everyone mad keen to assume its trappings. Because science goes outside the everyday, its results can be astonishing in the way the everyday is not. And people were suckers for the astonishing. But science was astonishing precisely because of a relation with the mundane. Science presupposes the everyday. Things that weren't scientific, human endeavors as opposed to abstracted and hence inhuman entities, tried to play the game of science and instead produced arcane meta-worlds removed from life as lived, imitations of science rather than science, that were limited to an ever smaller group of initiates who had no connection with what people really do.

The practitioners of these increasingly arid enterprises confused the incidental qualities of science—the necessity of science to invent and use insider terms to refer to things not part of daily life—with science itself, and concluded that if they too used words understood by only a few, they too were doing science. When those who flaunt this jargon as a badge of their knowledge failed to receive the honor given to scientists, they became embittered at their not getting what they felt was their due, and retreated even further into their mystical rites for initiates only.

A child's Superman costume doesn't mean he can jump tall buildings at a single bound, and a literature professor claiming she does "research" by emphasizing an aspect of a novel that she feels has been overlooked while citing a handful of fashionable thinkers isn't contributing to a store of objective knowledge, just sharing her thought processes, the way Gertrude Stein's "write down whatever goes through my head today" literary streams, on which she slapped the labels of poems, plays, operas, and novels, do. The vast majority of the world is too particular for science, including words. We need to recover this fact, be proud of it, and flaunt it. What we do outside of science is most of life. Why are we so keen to barter it away for the borrowed robes of something most of life will never be?

Social sciences are at the middle point where by definition there is both science and individuals, and hence close to equal amounts of impersonal science and personal application. They're unrelated except in combination: oil and vinegar don't mix, but you need both for the salad. For Weber, this merely meant constant discussion about their relationship in any given case.[2] But that implies constant involvement in the real world, and admission of fallibility or rejection of the impersonal based on personal objections—something that the professorate eager to buttress its own authority would not want to accept. So as Weber himself realized, the beating heart of what we may call, using his term, his own charismatic leadership, namely its admission of fallibility, was mummified into the pretense of purely objective science.

For an example, see the authority position of the Malinowski-era anthropologist, or its sackcloth and ashes Janus face, the breast-beating subservience of "write down as the last word what they say" school of contemporary post-Clifford Geertz attentiveness. Or the literary theory of structuralism, Derridean deconstruction, and Foucauldian power-exposure: I will show you what you have to see in this "text." Or the Janus face of this: you must be silent while I speak about this text because only I am a victim of type X or Y, and this is a text by a victim of my sort.

Weber knew that burning bodies of the religious comets in religion had long tails of much weaker epigones: the churches that they create. We are now in the period of the epigones well past the initial comets turning the prayer wheels of their "research" and disciplines—where the value of these "disciplines" is taken for granted, never justified.[3] But because the personal never goes away—it only remains unjustified and usually unarticulated—they left undiscussed the question, so important to Weber, of their application. This in turn meant professors were free to use this science in any way they chose with no justification—usually these days supporting those who were "marginalized" (as an active verb) by the evil power-holders.

The assumption nowadays seems to be that as a member of group X, your duty is to forward the interests of members of group X, which means make them more visible and attention-receiving than they are, so long as you, their defender, get to share their benefits. Latino/a professors teach LatinX literature, women teach

58 Abstraction

women's studies, gay men and women teach Queer Literature. Note that anthropology has largely been replaced by its domestic version of attention to groups inside our world, not outside. Yet this cheerleading for specific groups of which the cheerleader is a member (and if the cheerleader is not a member, woe betide him-her-them) is never justified—it's personal, after all. Instead, what's offered is the jargon of the "scientific" analysis of texts. This is contradictory: it's a scientific view of texts justified as subjectively true. Academic humanities and social sciences became irrelevant in the late twentieth and now twenty-first centuries by splitting into the two points of view that for Weber were intrinsically mixed together if not ever unified, science and personal.

Language is something human, and the more abstractly we consider it, the less useful such considerations become for actually changing anything. We just get further from the level on which it operates. A scientific view of language can't help us choose the right word, or sound more erudite, prove our point or diverge from it, be (perhaps unknowingly) too wordy or too elliptical, or know when to apologize or when to say nothing at all, because it is removed from the fact that all language is something we cause to come to be with each utterance. But we do this by choosing from things available to us. We are both master and servant of language. Yes, it's confusing. Because we are human, we don't need consideration of the human enterprise of language from a scientific perspective; it can't change what we do. All it can do is make us aware of the reality of how we live. Worse, the (quasi-)scientific view of language becomes a power tool of intellectuals, never linking back to the world—unlike science, whose conclusions can ultimately intersect the world again.

This is true to the extent that we scientize anything involving people: the scientific aspect peels off from the human. Thus the social sciences separate into the two divergent fates either of being misused or of becoming irrelevant. In fact, Weber was exceptional in pleading for objectivity (irrelevance) in the academic's pursuit ("The Scholar's Work") rather than using abstractions as power plays in the real world, as pioneers of this way of thinking such as Marx and Freud attempted to do, or the logical positivists out to kill moralizing and metaphysics, or the literature professors of our day intent on showing students the correct way to respond to a "text."

The attempt to scientize human endeavors almost always has as its end the goal of control, because it presents truths nobody is supposed to contradict. From these are drawn most typically conclusions about what people are to do—revolution, say, for Marx, or doing what Dr. Freud told them to do (as well as agreeing with him). If there ever was an intellectual bully it was Freud—which may be why he specialized in female patients; men probably wouldn't have put up with him and women hadn't yet realized they didn't have to do so. Or abandoning metaphysics, or spending your time drawing Lévi-Strauss's repetitive semiotic squares, or finding Derrida delicious rather than trivial, or marching in a parade for LatinX or Dominican or Boricuan literature.

The scientific aspect of the social sciences conveyed prestige and power on the people who used these for personal interpretations and goals. In the social sciences, there is no such thing as pure science: it's all for a personal goal, a fact which

Weber sometimes accepted and sometimes resisted. But why should individuals give up personal control over what they read and look at, largely in the personal realm? We can almost understand someone lecturing us about what we buy and how we live, but about what we read and look at? That seems a bridge too far. And that's where we are now. Too far.

Twentieth-century academics were (and are) enamored of Saussure, late Wittgenstein, and Derrida, considering language and its products as a system abstracted from the point of view (which doesn't mean "intention") of the individuals using it. That's the quasi-scientific aspect of the consideration by people whose livelihood is based on others' words: the philosophy they adopt reflects their own group's position, not the world as a whole—which probably cannot be conceptualized, as it consists of ever-changing particulars, perhaps ever repeating but also ever new. (This is where the Biblical book of Ecclesiastes sees only half the picture: that there is nothing new under the sun. From the perspective of the individual, this isn't true at all—for the individual, everything is new.)

Because Modernism is the point of view of a priestly caste, it generates me-too acolytes. But finally, it is doomed to be too closely identified with the specific group that finds it congenial. Never has academia (or the arts scene) seemed more irrelevant to actual life outside the ivory tower than in the second half of the twentieth and beginning of the twenty-first centuries. Academics and intellectuals (and their related fellow travelers, such as journalists) talk in one way, and non-academics in another. The famous split between high and low culture that has characterized the last century was written into the content of Modernism, as was the attempt to bring low culture into the purview of high (Warhol! Cultural studies about comic books! Exhibitions of motorcycles in the Guggenheim!). But the more fundamental contrast was between the abstraction of Modernism and the particulars of everyday life, not Rembrandt vs. comic books, or the *Medici Venus* vs. Barbie. The rise of backlash populism against the "elites" in the West in the twenty-first century seems at least partly explicable as a result of the cultural attitudes of Modernism that produced in those who held them a feeling of clubby insidership and superiority: we know things you don't. The world for the adherents of Modernist ideals was no longer about all people but only about insiders, who had separated from the vast multitudes of outsiders. And nobody likes feeling like an outsider; resentment is the inevitable result.

Notes

1 Popper, *The Logic of Scientific Discovery*.
2 Weber, "Basic Sociological Concepts."
3 Weber, "Introduction to the Economic Ethics of World Religions."

8

OFFENDED? YOU WIN!

Things grow strange at the bitter end of Modernism, past Postmodernism, when we see the elevation of individual viewpoints no longer offered as individual, but instead, each offered as the ultimate abstraction. The Romantic emphasis on the sensibility of artists, a very small number of people, has become generalized, so that whatever I among multitudes think to be so, is so. Unfortunately, that goes for everybody else as well. This is the emphasis on individual viewpoints given voice by what is usually called the second-wave feminism of the 1960s, which privileged sensibility over rationality, and has now been weaponized. If I am offended by X, then it's your responsibility to remove X: there is no retort possible once I announce what my view of events is. Words rule. Only they don't, because it's you who are causing those words. They're your words, sure. But I'm here too. And I also have the power of words, and of silence.

The basis of Enlightenment thought was the assumption that individuals had to interact with each other and hash out differences to create a whole. It opposed what Sir Francis Bacon, in his *Essays*, called the Idols of the Tribe, beliefs rather than justified assertions, as well as absolute monarchy, where one person controls everyone else. This Enlightenment thought necessitated the emphasis on reason, the mechanism of adjudicating between individuals, and the political system of democracy that offers a structure to resolve differences. Monarchy and other absolutisms such as that of a church do not require reason, only obedience to a set of rules external to all but a few people, or even to a single one (this led to clashes in the Middle Ages between pope and kings, and also to Henry VIII's Protestantism). If people merely do as they are told, they don't need to adjudicate differences, because the only difference possible is failure to obey the absolute rules, which is punished.

Similarly, Romanticism develops the sensibility of an individual, and assumes this will find echoes in everyone else. The possibility of conflict and hence the need for

DOI: 10.4324/9781003217688-10

resolution is not discussed. Modernism takes a deep dive into the self, by erasing the line between the creator and the world: the work is presented by the creator now standing invisible behind it, but the assumption is still that *hoi polloi* will work to understand it. Indeed, the claim of Modernist theory is that this is necessary to understanding the world. Art makes the stone stony, as Victor Shklovsky put it in 1917—a claim advanced a century before by the Romantic Shelley in his "Defense of Poesy," who held that poetry tore the veil of habit from the world and made us perceive it afresh.[1] Without art, we have no access to the world. This, of course, is nonsense.

The problem with the necessarily abstract, necessarily complex Modernist artwork that offered an alternative to the world itself was that it took so much work to enter—for most people, too much work. Hard works encouraged their makers to make even harder ones. Some people are willing to be instructed by a professor to make it through Joyce's *Ulysses*, but *Finnegans Wake* has been correctly described as being a work for PhDs with nothing better to do with their time. A handful of students read Imagist works of the young Ezra Pound and perhaps "Hugh Selwyn Mauberley," but nobody can make it through the *Cantos*. Few people have finished Proust's *In Search of Lost Time*, and nobody has read more than a handful of pages Gertrude Stein wrote, aside from her so-ballsy-it's-fun *Autobiography of Alice B. Toklas*. And Musil never finished *The Man Without Qualities* because by the time he got to the second volume and the Agatha story, he was apparently making it up a chapter at a time with no over-arching pattern, much as Stein past her early breakthrough work is just jottings of what occurred to her. Pure abstraction is the same as pure solipsism.

The Modernists seem to have been convinced that people had to follow them: their belief was in the necessity of their work more than their personal genius, and Postmodernism continues this assumption that everyone else is obliged to give attention to the work. Almost all Postmodernist art is the logical next step past the solipsistic abstraction of Joyce or Stein—which is why so much theoretical interest was thrown Stein's way in the heyday of Postmodernism. It's the ultimate expansion of one person's sensibility to create a whole landscape. But why should we look at what seem to be political slogans in neon? Fat in vitrines? A piece of what seems a factory machine? They seem like versions of the world outside the museum—why should we bother? Oh, say the artists! Because it transformed the world to art and you must appreciate!

And this is the connection of street protests to post-Postmodernism. One facet of academic Postmodernism was the rejection of the Enlightenment structures (rationality, debate, democracy) if they conflicted with personal sensibility. This was justified in terms of righting historic wrongs, defending weaker groups against stronger—and hence was a version of Marcuse's Marxism: if we allow rational discussion, we don't know what the outcome will be, and we can't allow a competition that might not end in our favor.[2] Feminism led the way: rationality was a power tool of the phallocracy; women were all about sensibility. This was a re-evocation of the valence of the nineteenth century placed on the identical dichotomy holding that men were the rational sex, women the emotional. Now the dichotomy is the same, it's just that women are the better ones. It's like the way gay rights groups have reclaimed the once derogatory term "queer" as a term of pride, or the way black rappers throw around what is called the n-word.

The Romantic artwork became abstract in Modernism and then Postmodernism, and then was given over entire to each individual, now claiming the power to have his, her, or their subjective point of view expand to the point where it merges with the objective. The distinction between subjective and objective is meaningless if each person demands the ability to be the universe, an expansion of the one into the whole seemingly prefigured by Emerson's image of the individual eye expanding to encompass the *Weltall*.

Each person being the center of all things means we are without any mechanism for adjudicating differences between people, because each person has expanded to the size of the universe. The opposites of single and collective no longer exist, because the collective no longer exists as an agglomeration of individuals. Instead, each individual claims to be the whole. We have neither the Hobbesian single head that determines the actions of the limbs, nor the cluster of discussing individuals of democracy. We have nothing to prevent the war of all against all. There is no such thing as discussion, there is only the attempt to impose the individual will on the grounds that it is not individual at all; not collective, but universal. I am offended by X or Y, so off with its head!

There is some semblance of order produced by claims of greater victimization: listen to me and not the others because I am the greater victim. But this presupposes agreement on the scale of victimhood. The weakness of this position is shown by the fact that those held to be victimizing them have to agree to this scale that gives victims moral clout: some do, but others don't. If the others don't, all the self-announced greater victims can do is fume: more words.

This strange progression that resulted in our current state of affairs bears repeating. Romanticism emphasized feelings, passion, and sensibility against the rationalism of the Enlightenment and neo-Classical period—but it kept the bar high to their expression, allowing only the greatest of individuals such expression, what were called creators, people (usually men) of genius. The greatest artworks were held to speak to, and for, all: all of us were to be in awe of the products of the few geniuses among us. So Romanticism was the generalizing of a few select individuals to offer access to the multitudes. It was therefore undeniably elitist, and pointed us back to a few extraordinary individuals to do our feeling for us.

Modernism was equally elitist. The products of Romantic genius were at least personal to the genius who created them, recognizably human. Modernism kept the idea of genius but stirred it into the work, which expanded to engulf the world. For Romanticism, the work was important because it expressed the genius of the creator; the Modernist work no longer led back to an identifiable individual, but only to itself, though the author (in whatever medium) was held to be the puppet master responsible for it all, if now behind the scenes. The Modernist work became central because of its abstraction—it no longer fit into the world, but replaced the world. Hence the difficulty of Modernist works. We no longer see

Offended? You Win! **63**

them as part of the world—representations of individual people or events like nineteenth century salon painting that made visually precise large topics like history, the Bible, and myth—but rather overarching views of all the world that hover above it.

The whole current movement of using offense as a weapon in colleges and in society—if I am offended the case is decided; no discussion; you will change, as I by definition have the upper hand based on my sense of offense—is part of this expansion of the subjective so that it swallows the objective. My immediate emotional reaction decides what has to happen for all. And so too street protests: this group wants X and Y to happen, and it will be done by force. Statues are the low-hanging fruit, as are store windows. Statues can be pulled down, and windows can be smashed and the clothes (say) in the window stolen. But that doesn't go very deep. And the more the protesters have to deal with something not in front of them that a few people armed with bats can't break, the harder it will be to achieve their goals. Systemic racism? A statue can be pulled down in a few minutes, but it's harder to define or effect deeper changes by force. And what changes are wanted? The deeper the perceived problem, the less the likelihood that changes can actually be effected, or for that matter even specified. We just want things to be different than they are! Well, OK.

The contrast between emotion, something we all have immediately, and rationality, what we have to work at, is actually created by the contrast between the single self and others, not the reverse. The abstraction of Modernism, derived from the celebration of the subjectivity of a handful of geniuses in Romanticism, was always a rebellion against the Enlightenment's acceptance that each of us had to take a number and wait our turn in a larger structure than that of our own sensibility. And street protests to ensure that subjective viewpoints of a small group prevail are the last stage of this progression of Romanticism-Modernism-Postmodernism.

Will we swing back to the Enlightenment assumption that we are part of a larger whole? This will send the pendulum back to reason. Or is each person the ultimate authority, claiming the democratization of the emphasis on emotion and sensibility of Romanticism and beyond? The victim sensibility produced in academia in late Postmodernism can end by the destruction of, among other institutions (and institutions always presuppose an emphasis on the group, not the primacy of the individual), academia. Going with the way things seem to you is a game for the pampered few when it takes place in, say, gender studies departments, and yet it is what destroys gender studies departments when students are encouraged to weaponize it against faculty, or when it spills into the street.

Academia is destroyed if (as it has begun to be) the "each person is king" mentality of post-Postmodernism spreads from being the power play of younger faculty members on older to being the power play of students on faculty. The basis of academia is similar to the assumption of the military: there are two groups of people, one that leads (officers/faculty) and one that follows (enlisted/students). Students by definition are to offer deference to faculty: they are there to learn. More successful faculty members, like more successful officers, do not insist on this

64 Abstraction

distinction between leader and follower, but take it as offered and carry on given that assumption. But this only works if the enlisted/students offer the deference presupposed by the system.

What happens when students insist that their subjective point of view is primary over what is being offered by the faculty member, that the person to change is not the younger but the older, the student in charge rather than the teacher? The system collapses, as it does in the military if the enlisted assume the position of deciders. And in its death throes, Modernism has placed us in this position. In the military, the currency is actions—the enlisted follow orders—and in academia, the currency is words—who "controls the narrative," as those who would like to control it (but don't) put it. The funny thing is, those held to "control the narrative" don't see themselves as being wordsmiths at all, but actors. And those trying to seize power don't want a change of action—as if they were like the *Bounty* mutineers seeking to stop Captain Bligh's sadism, who sought refuge beyond the arm of English law on the mis-charted and hence inaccessible Pitcairn Island—but only of words. Students demand to hear X and Y in classes, to have faculty members say Z—they don't want to flee, or to teach.

Tearing down a statue is easy—it's just a statue, it wasn't there before, and it doesn't have to be there after. But when you start saying that the goal is not a statue or even a different view of policing (say rolling back the militarization of US police) but instead changing cultural attitudes towards race or gender or making sure all groups (defined by what? skin color?) have the same average income (?) savings (?) as the highest-earning one (for example), then this takes us out of the realm of personal sensibility or offense into the social realm where we have to deal with many different groups. And there, it may not be so easy for individual sensibility to carry the day. Maybe we need rationality after all?

Notes

1 Shklovsky, "Art as Technique."
2 Marcuse, "Repressive Tolerance."

9

LIFE AFTER MODERNISM

We speak of the Cambrian explosion of hundreds of millions of years ago that produced most of our multi-celled organisms. Similarly, we can speak of the (by more limited standards) equally fertile Modernist explosion. Academics after the Modernist explosion withdrew into the ivory tower and abandoned the idea that their job could be to help all the people confronted with the twists and turns of everyday life. So the key to getting this idea back is to move beyond Modernism as a way of thinking and a set of givens. Modernism is all but dead anyway, living on the fumes of its reputation. Yet it's what we have, and professors want to keep things that way.

The problem with Modernism is that it has abstracted itself into irrelevance—and there's nothing abstract about demonstrations with violence, broken windows and destruction of property and monuments, or police and tear gas. Yet the demand that a small group of individuals have the power to remove and destroy public monuments—that thousands walk by daily without a thought—because they find them objectionable is the logical last gasp of academic Modernism, the last step on the expansion of the subjectivity of the Romantic artist into the abstract alternative worlds of high Modernism and their trivialization into Postmodernism.

In his *Tractatus*, Wittgenstein expressed frustration with the doings of ethicists and metaphysicians, indeed with philosophy itself as an ongoing enterprise. *Just shut up*, he seems to say! If you can't say something that isn't hot air, be quiet. In something of this same vein, I want professors of the humanities and social sciences to give up the theory and the entities that subsume individual people under abstract rubrics. You don't have to write that article! Think about life instead! We can still have professors of the humanities and social sciences, if they have any students and if universities continue to hire them, but their job should be to make us all aware of what individuals do and how individual readers or perceivers (such as all of us are) can relate to the products of other individuals. Not to parrot your theories.

DOI: 10.4324/9781003217688-11

66 Abstraction

This is a position against abstractions and for particulars. So it might seem I am taking a position like Hume's questioning of science: only the individual case, not the general, exists. No. Hume was talking about generalizations in the non-human world. I am talking about generalizing from people, and people aren't objective events in the world.

If Hume had been talking about people rather than incidents in the objective world when he held that generalizations are created by amalgamating particulars (he said it was human nature to do this, but in fact it's not more fundamentally so than the countless other things we do), he'd have been right. This is so not because people have a different essence than the objective world (some people argue that we don't—so if this were a necessity, we would have to conclude that people were arguing an impossibility), but simply that we are people and doing the arguing or generalizing, which is something we would all agree on. The sun rising is outside of us, whereas saying "Good morning" or anything else (or not speaking when we can) is something only people do. So too is talking about the sun rising. We're not the same as the objective world simply because we're the ones making the distinction between subjective and objective. If there is no difference, there is no point in talking. Making the distinction is a human action. It's not necessary to hold that people have "free will," just that we talk and act and the world doesn't. You can't have a conversation with a stone. Or not have a conversation. Or smile at it. Or snub it. And planets and blood corpuscles don't care what we think of them.

The point of science is precisely that, by escaping the human, abstractions become unproblematic. The problem is how to make sure they escape the human—and then the further problem: how to re-connect them? However, my switch from abstract to particular does echo the rejection, by phenomenologists like Heidegger, of conceptualizers like Socrates, emphasizing the "thrownness" of life over crystalline structures. Yet the phenomenologists, no less than Socrates, were also offering a view of all people all the time, and I am focusing by contrast on the particularity of experience. We are something that sits on nothing (in our terms)—the cloud.

But why is it stranger to think that words and actions of people come from something that has no substance until we give it form and body than it is to think that we ourselves come from nothing, or that our life as individuals is preceded by a state that itself isn't alive? Of course, in scientific terms, abstractions, we are alive because a sperm met an egg and so on. The mystery comes from seeing ourselves not as scientific abstractions but as cases of one—which is why this line of thinking usually ends in some form of religious belief: we acknowledge the impossibility of understanding, and make this impossibility the basis for positing another layer beyond ourselves. Individuals are not scientific; that's the nature of things, and both are possibilities.

According to the phenomenologists, we whoosh through life whether or not we try to do so. My emphasis rather is on the fact that works and words, and indeed all human actions, have to be made. They are a Fred Flintstone car: he doesn't turn a key, he provides the locomotion. We can't see them only in the past tense, or presuppose them. They needn't have been at all, so why were they? And why were they as they are? The individual is not propelled or thrown through life, but rather sits and then moves, deciding what to do or say, or whether to speak or act at all. The individual is not chopped liver, as New Yorkers say.

Hume was therefore wrong about natural occurrences but right about people. This is so not because people have or don't have what we call "free will," it's because they are in the middle of being people. They have a point of view from inside the entity, not just outside, as we humans see natural events. If corpuscles made science about corpuscles, the same would be true. But they don't, and it isn't. It's people who make science about corpuscles, and who talk about people.

The closer contrast to the Modernist abstractions of the humanities and social sciences is not theoretical physics or mathematics, but the much more people-centered science of medicine, which, unlike contemporary humanities and social sciences, always comes back to the particular. Medicine gets theoretical and inhuman with the sole purpose of helping individuals get and stay healthy, or mitigating the effects of what we call disease—the negative exceptions to the state we are seeking to preserve. To look ahead a bit, we have to agree that it's better to be healthy than sick, or we fall into the trap laid by some acolytes of Foucault in saying that any label that denigrates something is suspect. This is turned into the insistence that states like deafness or autism are not exceptions to be addressed and mitigated, but rather normal variations that are to be accepted, or even celebrated—much the same way homosexuality went from being the unacceptable deviation from normalcy to being one "orientation" among many.

Both medicine and the humanities/social sciences deal with people. But under the influence of Modernist abstraction, the humanities and social sciences have reneged on their obligation to bend back to people. They're like medicine that's never used to help cure the sick. Serious artists and thinkers could actually be of use to the world, but currently aren't. They remain in their bubble, convinced that abstraction itself is its own end. Meanwhile, the rest of the world checks its Twitter feed, plays video games, or follows the Kardashians. This may be modern, but it's not Modernist or even Postmodernist. People checking their Twitter feed don't do it in rebellion against the Modernist high artwork espoused by the Frankfurt School—they do it because it's fun and it interests or at least amuses them.

Yet we could all use some general, albeit not scientific, consideration of our individual lives. Each of us deals with the facts of life that are new and strange. With childhood comes the need to find out who you are and what your strengths and weaknesses are. Then comes the process of coming to terms with the finitude of each individual (which of your dreams can be realized and which can't?), then probably finding a way to put food on the table and a roof over your head. Then usually negotiating the mating or pairing process, usually doing as good a job as possible with the production and rearing of offspring, dealing with the joys and heartbreak of their growing up and the challenge of ultimately letting them go. And finally, the acceptance with increasing age of not being able to do things you

68   Abstraction

once could do, the gradual losses that pile up towards death, and the finality of departure, the realization that after a certain point you will have no more influence, no more decisions to make. The world belongs to someone else.

Life is full of changes and challenges, problems that we have to solve for ourselves. What do I want? How can I get it? How do I keep it? That's the process of scaling the mountain. For many of us, there's a plateau at the top where we are at the height of our game, but this too is limited in duration. Not all of life is lived at the highest level of capability and strength, though that is what our fantasies of movies and popular novels usually suggest. And who even wants to think about the downside of life? We are more interested in the process up the mountain than the process down. Who is that old man/old woman in the mirror? All of us have had or will have that moment. How do we navigate this part of life? And then beyond.

All this process, first up the mountain and then down, typically comes as a surprise to each of us, because nobody has lived it until they live it. That's what an era beyond Modernism could help us with. If we had had non-abstracted, non-scientific exposure to art and philosophy, largely devoted to earlier people's experiences with this process, it wouldn't be such a surprise, because we'd know it's the human condition. Knowing about it beforehand would help us understand it and deal with it better when it happens to us.

That's what professors of art and philosophy and literature and sociology could help us with once we abandon Modernism, whether in classrooms or more popular venues. Instead of doing this, under the influence of Modernism, they devote their lives to doing "research" that is merely moving chess pieces around on an intellectual board (and that nobody reads—and why should they?), and writing articles attacking commentators read only by other commentators. And they teach students whom they visualize as being future versions of themselves. The joke here is that very few of these students will ever become professors, so what's the point of teaching them to do the same thing, which moreover is pointless?

Introductions to standard works of literature, that at least could present big topics for students to think about, have largely disappeared in academia, attacked as propping up the white male patriarchy, in favor of works turned by their presentation in classrooms into the propaganda tracts of splinter groups whose influence, for those not themselves members of these splinter groups, is limited to the duration of the course. What has seeped outside academia from classrooms such as this is the more general notion that any individual's response is immune to objections or revisions. And now it has upended academia by putting students in charge of who speaks, what is taught, who teaches it, and how. The logical end of Modernism is a war of all against all with no structure accepted for mediation, with its only connection to the world through the relatively narrow crack of the disaffected. Meanwhile, more mainstream students are ignored and have largely given up on such classes, as these classes have been turned into an echo chamber for social activists. The connection of the arts and literature to the world could be so much deeper and more general.

Students are not the only ones nowadays who think they have both the right and the obligation to object to what professors say. It's the parents too. Parents usually don't want their children to be changed if they have been brought up with certain givens. Education is all about getting people to question their assumptions and consider other points of view. Some parents, who reason that they are paying for what little Johnny or Susie hears, don't want this to happen, even if the student would be receptive. So professors are under attack from both right and left. What unifies these attacks is a largely general acceptance of the givens of late Modernism: subjective is objective. It's unclear if this view seeped out of academia or if it grew naturally outside academia. I'd say, for the left it's an academic influence. But the right, which never accepted much past the personal end of the scale anyway, is suddenly feeling vindicated as even toffs begin to speak their language. This may be at least one reason for the sudden explosion of what are called "populist" politicians in many countries, certainly the US and the UK.

PART III

The Spectrum of Disciplines

10
PERSONAL AND IMPERSONAL

Science is one end of a spectrum whose other end is the purely personal. At various places in between come philosophy and the arts as well as the academic humanities and social sciences. Everything we do is related, and things can change place on the scale. Science isn't scientific, people are scientific. We all allow unscientific things such as personal tastes and preferences (redheads over blondes, chocolate over vanilla, Mahler over Bruckner) in individuals—which is to say, we don't ask that they be generalizable. This is the case not because they can't be, but because nobody is interested enough in them to ask that this be done. If we demand that they be seen as apersonal generalities, we can set about a way to do so—which doesn't mean we will succeed soon, or ever. Yet by seeing them as potentially scientific, we have hauled them out of the darkness of the personal, where we don't look because we don't care. Suddenly (for whatever reason) we care. Until this point, my preference for (say) chocolate over vanilla had no meaning or interest for anyone but me. Suddenly, for whatever reason, it does. Let's say vanilla beans are suddenly a political issue. Eating meat becomes problematic. Recycling or not. Suddenly we look at things we hadn't looked at. And the looking changes its nature.

Thus disagreement is baked into human interactions because the spectrum doesn't determine where things are meant to go. Even at the impersonal and scientific end of the scale, personal objections are possible, like "research into IQ is elitist" or "finding a 'gay gene' would help/hurt the situation of gay people" or "Nazi racial science wasn't science at all." Or "paleontology is against God's will." This insists that statements held to be at the impersonal end of the spectrum aren't actually so. If the content of what was taken to be scientific is asserted to be personal, it is, to that degree and by those who see it as personal, demoted as science and is moved along the scale toward the personal end.

Cases such as these that attempt to (so to say) fold one end of the scale, the personal, up to meet the other, the scientific, are the most extreme. But anything

DOI: 10.4324/9781003217688-13

74 The Spectrum of Disciplines

on the scale moving toward the scientific impersonal—which means the middle of the scale, the happy hunting ground of twentieth century academia—can be objected to on personal grounds. This is so because objectors are always people: individuals are the ones constructing edifices of the impersonal. Abstractions don't posit people; people posit abstractions. This means the social sciences are always vulnerable to objections, and also the humanities to the extent that these approach the social. The objection is always the same, Hume's perception that you can't justify a general by collating particulars, just make things that seem to describe the world—which he called human nature, implying wrongly that this was an unavoidable weakness, and hence illegitimate. Of course, it isn't illegitimate at all: I'm going to look in the fridge for the milk, where it will be unless it's been left out—and that doesn't happen often enough for me to assume I will have to look in two places. If it's never in the fridge, I don't look there at all. That's knowledge (i.e. "human nature") too. Also that when it snows more than an inch or two I'll probably have to shovel, and that P. G. Wodehouse almost always puts me in a good mood, and that a glass will hold the water I put in it—unless. Unless what? It's cracked, or it—I don't know. You tell me. What other reason could a glass fail to hold water—and earthquakes don't count. Just because I can't think of any other reason, I can't say there aren't any.

Most of what lets us function in the world is knowledge of this "generally true" order. Science isn't different, it's just further along the scale towards "I don't even have to think of alternatives because I've eliminated all the obvious ones and most of the arcane ones, which doesn't mean there isn't an even more arcane one I haven't thought of, but the probability of this is so small that I don't have to add it to my checklist." Which doesn't mean it couldn't happen. The rocket could explode despite all we know and our using best scientific practices developing it. Planes fly unless—I don't know, we just have to explain after the fact if they don't: a missing bolt? Strange updrafts? A kamikaze pilot? Hijackers?

The tendency of the social sciences, in order to justify themselves as disciplines, is to arrive at causal links from correlation: the fact that X% of group Y does A or B is a fact about that group, and applies to all or virtually all of its members. This always contrasts with the fact that individuals remain individuals. And it's these individuals who produce the entire scale. Objections to this creeping scientization of people can come from either the political right or left, depending on whether the general statement about the group is positive or negative and how the objectors as individuals feel about the members of that group. For example, the facts about average American black educational levels or test scores, expressed as facts about the group (if defined in racial terms), can be attacked by either right or left if held to be qualities of the group rather than individuals being determined by other factors—such as housing, "systemic racism," school quality and/or parental involvement (or its lack), or nutrition. Here it's the left insisting on breaking apart a group into individuals that can be individually affected. The right will object if told that the group determines the future of its individual members. Just work hard in school! Accept Jesus Christ as your personal Savior! Presumably it was this

Personal and Impersonal **75**

subsuming of individuals into groups that Margaret Thatcher was rejecting when she held that "there is no such thing as society." And of course she's right to the extent that society presupposes the individuals articulating it.

The social sciences don't have to make such absolute quasi-statements to which a single individual can serve as a counter-example; they can be more toward the center of the scale or even close to the personal, suggesting that perhaps there is some connection but we don't quite know what. But this kind of observation doesn't make headlines, and it doesn't justify calling something a discipline for academic purposes. And it won't get a sociologist tenure—though this is increasingly a moot point as humanities and social science students disappear in universities and the dearth of jobs in these fields means, in the long run, that these simply cease to exist as fields and go back to being what they were before. Namely, things amateurs could do at their leisure, rather the way philosophy was before it was academized. And that means more individualized, probably quirkier. How would the world be poorer? Granted, it would be independently wealthy people who could do this, and so fewer, or people who could get the wealthy to support them if they did it full time. But who says it has to be full time? And what's certain is that almost nothing of what academics do seeps outside the ivory tower. (The big exception for liberals in the twentieth century is probably John Rawls's conception of material equality for all being the only just/acceptable situation.)[1]

The intrinsic tension for the area in the middle between the pull to the scientific end of the scale and the personal is clearest nowadays, and most vicious when expressed in terms of identity politics. This is an interesting phenomenon because it attempts to combine these two magnetic poles. That's why "Speaking as a X (LatinX, Gay woman, Queer Black male), I…" is the form for this combination of individual and group. I am speaking, hence individually, but am doing so in my capacity as someone to whom generals that escape my individuality apply. This is not the same as saying that a group has voted individually and elected me their spokesperson, an individual expressing things a group of individuals have agreed on. As a (say) LatinX, I claim direct knowledge of this general LatinXness. In Platonic terms, I have contemplated the Idea and need no one else's input.

But because individual and general are contradictory, they can only be combined when their oil and vinegar combination is contrasted to something outside of them—the carafe that contains them. And this has to be a different sort of thing from the contents. The contrast to this amalgamation of individual and group is invariably the majority seen as oppressive. Nobody can get away with saying, "Speaking as a straight white male, I…" because straight white males are held to be individuals for which the general is secondary. Members of the group held to be in power speak for themselves, and hence as individuals, not for the group. The group doesn't want anything because the individuals have it already.

So this combination of individual and group that is the basis of our current identity politics bears out Weber's realization that all quasi-scientific statements in the social sciences are produced for individual reasons: it's intrinsically a position taken by people who feel their lot is unfair. The victimization sweepstakes of our

76 The Spectrum of Disciplines

day produces the structure of academic thought in the middle part of the scale. If individuals don't feel victimized, they don't wield the general as a weapon—note again, the group is an entity at a more abstract level than the individual. If they were merely a collection of individuals, it would be reasonable to demand of them that they act as individuals—work hard, stay in school, obey the law, and so on. And that is what the majority against which they are reacting typically demands. Because the demand of the group that sees itself as disprivileged insists that its groupness is real and is not individual, this seems to miss the point to them—and to be evidence of more oppression.

It's for this reason that academic humanities and social sciences have been so altered at the end of Modernism by representatives of what call themselves marginalized groups. (Marginal perhaps, but "marginalized" means they were once part of the text and have been pushed to the side to the blank space—they were made marginal—and this is not what they typically claim.) Namely that it's these groups with the strongest allegiance to the quasi-scientific end of the spectrum, which is the basis of the academic humanities and social sciences. This fragmentation of generals is an interesting last-ditch effort to shore up the crumbling walls of the consideration of individuals in general terms that Modernism bequeathed us.

Identity politics are an attempt to re-scientize the personal, a late and ultimately futile attempt to pump some blood back into the feeble body of the Modernist patient. They didn't come out of nowhere. They're the logical working out of the Modernist creation of academic disciplines in the center of the scale. The professorial defenders of identity politics have become some of the bitterest defenders of academia in its dying days of few students and almost no jobs. It seems paradoxical that self-professed powerless outsiders should wield so bluntly the power of institutions. And now with students, usually at elite institutions, brandishing the weapons of embittered outsidership and demanding, usually successfully, that powerful institutions back them up, we have reached the final waltz in the all but deserted ballroom of Modernism.

This is an attack on the individual in the name of the group. It is the opposite of the attacks by individuals on institutions even as solid as science. The assertion that science isn't science but subject to personal response is a personal assertion, at least for the person making it—so they will be as offended by your saying their response isn't appropriate as they would be if a stranger told them that they didn't in fact prefer chocolate to vanilla. How would the stranger know? The scale doesn't prevent arguments. How could it? It's just an ordering of what we do, and disagreement is something we do. (I would summarize Wittgenstein, early and late, a Modernist thinker if there ever was one, as trying to eliminate human disagreement, distancing himself from the sweaty agon of actual human life and existing only on the abstract level, whether these are states of affairs or language games, like sketching a river on a map rather than being in the rushing waters.)

This is also the scale of what we call most subjective to most objective—and individuals use words to describe it, though it is situated in the world. So if someone says, Aha! You are saying the objective world is created by words!, this is

Personal and Impersonal 77

no more true than saying that it is through words we express the world. It's there outside of words. Here, I am writing English. But that doesn't mean English creates the world, nor me (because I am the one using it), nor this chapter. We get to pick what to focus on, or at least change focus. Focus on language is only one focus.

At one end of the scale, the yin of individual response is huge and the yang of objectivity is minimal; at the other end, the reverse is true. But neither the yin nor the yang completely goes away, whichever end of the scale we are at. It should not have been earth-shaking to realize that even statements of personal taste or what we call "mental states" are subject to social response or correction. You eat meat or use throw-away plastic? How irresponsible! (People whose world is centered around themselves take great umbrage at this.) Science as an activity is not invalid because it turns out (surprise!) that scientists have to decide to turn their attention to a specific topic and have personal views on whether this subject is worthwhile/moral/godly. Christianity is not invalidated because the Shroud of Turin turns out to be a medieval fake; this particular instantiation of it may be, but religion is a place on the spectrum, not a set of particular beliefs. And discovering that an objective thinker is of a particular political persuasion does not automatically invalidate that person's work. It might do so, of course—as, for example, we consider racial or Nazi "science" bogus. But discovering that (say) a doctor is of one political party or another doesn't mean their advice is necessarily about furthering the aims of that party, or that the nationality or gender of a scientist is what's behind the pronouncements of that person. We can discover that it is or does, but that is a different point. Saying that some degree of personal can creep into even the objective end of the spectrum doesn't mean that there is no such thing as that end of the scale. We (or a subset of "we") simply move(s) statements to a different place on the scale as we (or its subset) discover(s) their aspects that are more or less social and collective—that part of the scale doesn't cease to exist. Where on the scale something belongs is not subject to adjudication by the scale itself; there will always be disagreements between people regarding where statements belong. The delineations on the scale are not of specific utterances, but of how they function.

But the scale is composed only of these specific things—it's not a credenza that exists separately from the things it orders, nor even a string of pearls: there's no thread. "We" "decide"—we can equally well say that the world shows itself to be as it is. What stands behind words is itself not committed to any one set of words over the other. We are always doing a specific thing, but one of those specific things can be talking about doing a specific thing, or how specific things relate to each other. One end of the spectrum doesn't explain the other, and we can operate at multiple positions on the spectrum in quick succession. A nuclear scientist can turn away from her calculations and wonder when it's going to be lunchtime, watch a bird out the window, speak to a colleague about the weather, call home, and then turn back to her work.

We can object to kicking into scientific mode, but we rarely argue any more that doing so is illegitimate—just wrong. We can't justify an abstraction based on

78 The Spectrum of Disciplines

aggregating individual cases (Hume). But what Hume failed to consider was the fact that we can simply switch our focus to the level of that abstraction, and work with it not in terms of particulars but in terms of the abstraction itself (constants, control groups, double blind studies, and so on—the techniques of science have to be learned). We didn't need Kant to justify science. We just do it, the same way we just decide what our long-term goals in life are rather than just asking what's for dinner: one is abstract, the other immediate. (NB: the distinction between particular and abstract is relative. "Money" is abstract with respect to dollar or pound sterling, but not with respect to medium of exchange.) Yet the fact that we can do it doesn't mean we should do it on everything all the time. Science is only one specific way of considering the world, at the abstract end of a spectrum of considerations ranging from concrete to general. The humanities, focused on the particular works of particular humans, are perfectly fine without science, as are words and other human actions.

Another way of seeing this spectrum of personal/individual to abstract/scientific is this: at one end of the spectrum are the utterances that almost no one else is in a position to contest and at the other end are things all those we are speaking to who can play the game we are playing can respond to. The most immune seem to be things like: I feel as if I have to throw up. Or: I am really enjoying this ice cream! Nobody, it seems, can tell us we are wrong. Others can't say, You do *not* like that ice cream! Or rather only someone who knows us intimately can say this, and playfully—and we can respond by saying, Yes I do, I've just discovered! The other person can't take on the assertion of taste itself, just the likelihood that it's a serious assertion.

People who are advocates of one end of the scale or the other frequently want to apply the POV of their end to others, what I call folding one end of the scale up to touch the other. We are most familiar with the attempt of those for whom the personal side of things dominates—nobody can tell me I don't like this ice cream, or that I have the right to drive at any speed, or own all the guns I want—to apply this also to science, as if they simply didn't understand that science is fundamentally something different than the way the world seems to an individual. They believe X or Y because it's in the Bible, or a celebrity said it, or they heard it on a television program. They frustrate others with different views because the personal end of the scale is not made to tolerate other views. And it stands to reason that the personal people would feel that the whole world is against them.

They aren't completely wrong, because people at the other end of the spectrum are equally determined to apply their criteria for statements that don't involve personal viewpoints. This is the whole arsenal of what is called logical thinking, perhaps best summarized by Carl Sagan as "baloney busters," starting with the fallacies of the ancients: ad hominem reasoning (I don't like this person so what is coming out of their mouth is wrong), excluded middle (if you don't come see me it must be because you hate me), appeal to authority (she's the boss so she must be right), straw man (liberals are trying to castrate us by instituting checks for gun purchasers), slippery slope (taking away our guns leads to taking away our houses),

Personal and Impersonal **79**

and so on.[2] If your view is one where people exist as discrete individuals spaced out six feet apart (as we were supposed to be in the coronavirus pandemic), then all the tools of what we call logic are necessary to re-unite them. What frustrated scientists fail to see is that this is not necessary for someone for whom the world does not consist of discrete individuals standing six feet apart who have to be reunited, but rather a world with themselves at the center that radiates out to include others already in relation to them whose importance decreases as the circles widen.

I have a good deal of sympathy for this view because much of our life gets its power from this personal end of the spectrum. Gerard Manley Hopkins dedicated his harrowing poem about "The Wreck of the Deutschland" as follows:

> To the happy memory of five Franciscan Nuns, exiled by the Falk Laws, drowned between midnight and morning of Dec. 7th, 1875.

And it begins:

> Thou mastering me
> God! giver of breath and bread;
> World's strand, sway of the sea;
> Lord of living and dead;
> Thou hast bound bones & veins in me, fastened me flesh,
> And after it almost unmade, what with dread,
> Thy doing: and dost thou touch me afresh?
> Over again I feel thy finger and find thee.

If you're drowning in cold water in the night next to a listing hulk, you'd better see yourself in a one-on-one relationship with God: science isn't going to help much. The *happy* memory, mind you. When you're drowning, everything but you and the creator falls away.

Without the personal too, devotion to family is impossible—and indeed some thinkers insist that we should treat our parents or our offspring no differently than we consider every living human being, even the ones we don't know. But most of us just can't pull this off. And how would we feel about achieving the same parity by demoting those close to us and being indifferent to all?

The impersonal end of the spectrum can be taught, and usually has to be. Very little college time is spent on encouraging people to go with their specific circumstances, what we call prejudice and superstition as well as all the Idols of the Tribe—we all have those already. And the point of education is to help us get along with others, so suddenly we have to use what we call reason and logic to communicate with those who are not part of our extended personal bubble. College is about a group experience, after all—or one-on-one with a tutor who guides you. It's quite true therefore that education is not neutral—its point is precisely to solve a set of problems that simply don't arise if you live comfortably in your

80 The Spectrum of Disciplines

bubble. And this point is frequently made by those who reject the need for and the effects of education: it really is foreign, and whatever it is, it's not neutral—what we call logic, as if it's possible to think illogically, or as if "illogical" is merely a non-being rather than a substantial something else.

The social contract theorists of the eighteenth century postulated a world before society that lacked laws and opposed it to what they saw. This produced the rabbit hole of imagining that what we have was constructed somehow from something else. In fact, the contrast between the state of nature and the state of society is a contrast not between two times, a before and an after, but internal to something that is both at the same time: people think in the way of the state of nature people even today—and not just some people, all of us. The question is only: what is the effect of doing this under X or Y circumstances? If everybody is bent on (say) shooting at everybody else, we may well insist that we have to put a stop to it. Not because it's wrong or philosophically incorrect (again, Wittgenstein: there is no such thing as philosophy proving you wrong) but because we'd all be dead, the war of all against all of the social contract theorists such as Hobbes, who mistakenly concluded that absolute monarchy is the only alternative to this war of all against all.

The social contract theorists, all of whom stood in opposition to people who think in terms of themselves as the center of it all, assumed that we already were thinking in terms of groups; the question was merely whether this was necessary/good (Hobbes) or bad (Rousseau). But we all think in both ways at various times, and the conflicts arise between the attempts of one group of thinkers to convince the others. My sympathies for the possibility of personal worlds should be clear; equally clear should be my acceptance that these (for purely practical reasons) should be confined to the personal sphere of art and family, not to the group. That they wouldn't be so confined is what Isaiah Berlin feared in his numerous attacks on totalitarian states: the imposition of a single point of view on all. Those who have access to the inter-personal structures of science and logic are far more likely to also be able to appreciate things on the personal end of the spectrum than someone who lives in an enclave of like-minded people who see the world as conspiring against them is to be able to be swayed by alternative viewpoints.

Of course, the personal bubble can be quite a sophisticated bubble. Many artists live in a world of their own, for example, and someone like Proust is the poet of that individual point of view: everybody is a character in his sensibility. Indeed, painters create worlds where everybody in (say) Munch paintings looks alike, made of curves, just the way everybody in Edward Gorey's world, or Charles Addams's, looks generically similar. Or Poussin's. Or Vermeer's. It's not reality at all. Visitors to an art gallery see examples of one personal world after the next. Many visitors don't really see the point of this lineup. If all you have is your own personal world, you will also reject those of others. So of course there is a point in educating people to interact outside of their personal bubble rather than cushion themselves within it.

There's quite a distance from gun-waving protesters with Confederate flags to Proust and Munch—but there are also affinities. All are based on personal views of the world. However, the differences are found in the fact that a personal view of the world expressed in art does not threaten to take over the world of others. If you don't want to read Proust, or look at Munch, you don't, unless you have to fulfill a distribution requirement in college. And even then, you get it over with and move on. Besides, the number of people in colleges nowadays forced to give figures such as Proust or Munch even an unsuccessful try are very few. It seems that confining your personal view of things to art is the way socialized people (this is a sort of paradox) fit into the world—because of course the point of art is to in a sense escape socialization, create your own world. Only it doesn't force others to enter it. The same is true of any artist—writers, for example. Creating your own world doesn't mean you're a freak or live outside the world. Where we need to worry (here I agree with Berlin) is where those with their own personal world-view impose it on others—a Mussolini, for example, or more contemporary examples. Or a Mao, a Stalin, a Lenin. But those with the personal world-view will see those with the more social view as imposing their view too—as indeed they are.

Education into the ways of science and logic is necessary if we are not to be at each other's throats (state of contemporary nature)—but it does change people. Should it? Not because education is morally better: it's just necessary for allowing groups of people to get along. We can't use "logic" to convince someone who insists on the primacy of belief or authority. That's like thinking that speaking our language slowly and distinctly to someone who doesn't speak it will make them understand. Logic is a thing in the world, not the structure of the world. So how do you bridge this divide between what we call logic (which is a series of ways to exist peacefully with divergent others) and belief (which is all about the self and like-minded others)? Lots of ways. Bribes, punishments, "nudges," sending out a personable spokesman/woman: there are lots of things that work. Maybe. Sometimes. What almost certainly won't work is more logic. And assuming that logic will work in areas where it's not in force is the error of educated people. Logic is the language of separated divergent individuals who have to work together. If you just insist that everybody mirror your view, you don't need logic, nor do you appeal to it. Probably you appeal to force.

I'm all for education. What I'm not for is the failure of the educated to see that their point of view is a specific one with its specific presuppositions: those who don't share these are not merely aberrations that must be resisted or stamped out. This was apparently Wittgenstein's impatience with those who believed that logic could tell us things rather than merely codify what we know. We don't learn things with philosophical proofs, we just order our thoughts. Philosophy isn't a weapon. At least this is true among those who reason together, who accept the rules of the common game. It certainly is wielded as a weapon against those who refuse to take part in the enterprise itself, which is based on negotiating between discrete individuals, and who instead see the world centered on themselves where the stone enters the water and others as arranged outwards in circles of decreasing importance. Scientists reject the "either you're with me or against me" world-view

82 The Spectrum of Disciplines

of, say, Christian conservatives or Islamic militants. For scientists, the world is not most primordially about people at all.

Social sciences, in the middle between individual human and generalized inhuman abstract, came to be from the direction of the end of the spectrum considering particulars. Their justification therefore consists in moving closer to the pole of science, insisting that we can understand the world of humans at the level of the abstract, not the level of the individual. Social sciences consider people as if they were corpuscles or stars and aim to achieve certainty, which is what makes them (even to a limited degree) like science. The degree of certainty proposed varies from writer to writer as well as the scientific unit—Marx asserts more certainty than Weber, for example—but all order people with no regard to their volition or personal views.

This is a fact about the level of consideration, not (once again) a statement about whether people are controlled or have free will. If we are looking at the general, say the effects of the institution of marriage, we can have ever so many caveats to our assertion, we are still saying that most or all individuals in this situation do or are X or Y. (If there are only a few, we can't make a theory out of it.) Yet the certainty of the human sciences, to the extent that it is postulated or achieved, is bought at the price of believing the world to be invariable and hence predictable. And predictable means boring. All certainty is gray; only life is green (to play off of Goethe's *Faust*.)

Thus it's arguable that (for example) it's Weber's own methodology that produced the portrait he offered of his age as soulless and bureaucratic, his filter determining the results because of what it filters out.[3] The very possibility of seeing social structures at all is based on the intuition that the people at the top of the pyramid are different from all the rest, who only exist to carry out the wishes of the few that they will never understand. This silent bureaucratic method of looking at human products is perhaps most characteristic for Weber not of the world of people falling in love, going for a run, or fixing dinner, but of Weber's own home world of academia, which, as he himself noted in "The Scholar's Work," is based on chance and ceaseless work for no visible end. His conclusions about the mechanistic soullessness of the modern age were written into his presuppositions, into his level of abstraction.

If there's no problem with our lived world, we rarely have recourse to science. If it ain't broke, we don't seek to fix it. Even Freud, one of the pioneers of theories about all individual people, was trying to fix psychological abnormalities, and medicine addresses illnesses: all take for granted a postulated pole of normal. Then something's amiss. Or something has changed. Or something caught our attention—which means a diversion from normal. Why people get sick is medicine; why people are born at all is religion or metaphysics, offering explanations for the normal, which suddenly seems to require explanation. But the reason for this apparent requirement for an explanation for the normal is personal: suddenly it seemed important to Sartre (for example) to ask why there is something rather than nothing. Most of us aren't worried by this. This is Weber's point that all objectivity

Personal and Impersonal **83**

in the social sciences, if it exists at all, is the result of subjective factors: something suddenly seems to us a problem.[4]

Thus the social sciences career between over-reach and under-reach. Over-reach is more exciting because it seems more important: Freud or Marx, all people do X or Y. Or: this study shows that people who do A or B are more C or D (say, racist/tolerant). Under-reach is where most of the social sciences have lodged since the pathbreakers: scientific studies that show that people respond 0.2 seconds faster to an image that is whatever than to an image that (in the view of the experiment) is not-whatever. But how to translate this to anything interesting, like saying that people who X or Y are more—let's say—racist? Difficult. The problem is the same as saying that rats fed a steady diet of A or B perform less well/better in a maze than those with lower doses/no dose. Was this the reason? More fundamentally, how does a study on laboratory rats translate to people, who presumably are exposed to a lot less of A or B and don't actually have to run through a literal maze? Even science has trouble translating the laboratory to real life (the theory says this astral body should do X or Y, but we've never seen it; the rocket should get to the moon, but will it?). How much more difficult it is for social science!

Science diverges from the everyday, is limited to the few, and uses these not-quotidian terms. That's just a side effect, not the point. For outsiders, however, these seem the defining characteristics, the way people unused to the conventions of the classical ballet imitate it by standing on tiptoe and twirling around. In something of the same spirit of unintentional caricature, literary scholars and artists believe that using jargon and long discipline-specific words among a group of insiders means what they are doing is scientific. But this is to confuse the means of science with its end. The purpose of science isn't to be arcane or limited to expensive laboratories, that's just the necessity of looking for explanations for phenomena outside the normal range of experience. For scholars of the humanities, by contrast, speaking an arcane language and creating a priestly caste that deman-ded respect was the point. But this is to science what twirling around on tiptoe is to *Swan Lake*. Science can change the world, but Modernist arts and scholarship only get further and further from the world.

In Modernist academia, the products of humans—books, words, artworks—are considered as if they were unconnected to people and formed a coherent manifold the way we say the objective world does. Of course, we can postulate that about any group of discrete objects or entities—say, the things on my desk. The scale I am sketching goes from the absolutely personal to the absolutely general, which we call objective. We can study things at any point along this scale. The things on my desk are too clearly things I put there, so I know there is no way I can pretend they are worthy of quasi-scientific study as an objective manifold. Because I put them there (I didn't put astral bodies or germs or fish where they are), seeing them as a coherent group of things to be investigated doesn't seem to have much point. (By contrast, if I were a Proust I might be able to get a Modernist novel out of these, but that is presented as merely my subjective utterance: read it if you choose, or not.) Similarly, people put their works, words, and actions in the world. The

84 The Spectrum of Disciplines

fact that what people do and produce can be studied as if an impersonal manifold doesn't make these studies have a point, because nobody outside of a small priestly caste cares.

For Modernism, however, this sort of activity seemed to make sense, because Modernism thought that we needed this priestly caste to explain the difficult works we'd be fighting to access. It turned out we aren't fighting to access these works— though in the early twentieth century it was a plausible assumption that we would. After all, people had accepted the Romantic notion of geniuses who would do our feeling for us. Why not Modernist artists and scholars who would Explain It All to Us? It didn't turn out that way. Modernism (or indeed any intellectual current) turned out to have a limited life span: initially exciting, then running out of steam as it became clear that its assumptions were not viable past a certain point because they ran into an ever-changing reality. And with Modernism almost out of gas, these activities of considering the product of humans as if they were objective manifolds seem an increasingly bizarre way to spend one's life.

We can generalize about people, or their actions, or their works. But these are things we do to keep ourselves amused and busy—not for that reason illegitimate (some people play solitaire to pass the time), but also not something creating a coherent picture of an extant whole that stands outside all of us, the way our postulate of an objective world does. Modernist humanities and social sciences hold these things to be research, like science. At the same time, abstractions from people that have come to seem inhuman—designations of race and gender—are held to be "socially constructed," and hence not more than subjective. The two extremes meet in the middle between objective and subjective, a middle that professors have staked out and can control. The attempt to merge the two ends of the spectrum where one end is science and the other a preference for vanilla over chocolate is held to be sophisticated, yet in fact it is like insisting that evolution is "only a theory," or that the idea that humans are influencing global warming is "unproven." There are degrees of proof, and provability. Some things are very well proven indeed. It may feel original and exhilarating to deny degrees of difference, but in fact it's intellectually destructive. Sometimes differences make a difference.

Similarly, there are degrees of certainty as there are degrees of subjectivity in concepts, and saying that gender is "constructed" doesn't necessarily mean it's flimsy and will fall down. The three little pigs built three houses in increasing degrees of solidity; the wolf found the first easy to blow down but the second much harder, and was unable to blow down the third. All were "constructed," and the nay-sayers to the increasing consensus about global warming are few and far between and diminishing. So saying that there is a social component to gender doesn't mean it can be blown down. Or for evolution: no, we don't have 100% proof, but we can have more proof or less; for evolution we have more. A lot more. Tarring taxonomies as all equally "constructed" obscures this fact.

The education industry is a powerful one. So as a bow to this fact, I note that it is perfectly possible to charge fees to usually younger and in any case less practiced

Personal and Impersonal **85**

people to take part in a classroom discussion of literature and the arts, or of writers like Weber or Popper or Freud or Nietzsche, without the pretense of there being disciplines to study them. Books allow us to get up close and personal with human experiences and discuss others in a way we cannot with real people standing before us, with whom we must interact based on our relationship with them. Reading a book is like watching porn: we owe them nothing, they aren't our mother or sister, just bodies. So look! That's what they are there for.

Or why appeal to porn? The *Venus de Milo* or Michelangelo's *David* or the *Discobolus of Myron*: what gorgeous bodies! They were made in marble for us to stare at. If they stood before us, we would have to orient ourselves towards them as people: am I allowed to look? What if they objected to our looking? Works of art and thought turn human flesh into marble or celluloid. We are not only allowed to get up close or stare, we are encouraged to do so. That's their allure. And their purpose. They take the human out of the web of relations in which real humans are caught—including us, the perceiver. It's the looking that's the point, and what we learn is up to us. Colleges could create the situation for this looking, and professors could guide it. The secret is for professors to remove themselves from the interaction as much as possible: facilitate it, sure. But then pull back. The Modernist conception of disciplines encourages the professor to insert herself boldly and as loudly as possible in the middle. This is unfortunate because (a) it ruins the point of reading the work, and besides, (b) the professor is almost always less interesting than the work.

Works could help us process our lives. What we know about the world, and ourselves, is in this middle part of the scale: we pay attention to what happens, and begin to form habits and ways of dealing with the world based on generalizations. It's not science, but it's how we process the world. We learn more about, say, sex, every day we live, or food preparation, our partner's moods, what the publishing world wants, or how politics works. These do not require disciplines, though people who do these things more intensively can give us vocabulary to create and understand our conceptualization. Under the best of circumstances, this is how the Modernist humanities and social sciences relate to students; unfortunately, this is rarely how they are presented.

Works and products of humans are the products of humans, and the touches of their fingers or the movements of their thought give the most interesting way to regard them, not considering them as dead things to be classified and studied. Neither do they require the interaction that is part of talking to a person in front of us. They are between living people and stones, their very existence the result of the shaping and forming by people, both their fundamental qualities and their surface. (In a painting, the painter's hand controls every stroke; in a photograph, the photographer chooses this arrangement of things among multiple takes, or recognizes a fortuitously perfect shot as the one to exhibit.) They are personal, but we can get as close to them as we want. And we don't have to abide by the social conventions we would if we were talking to the person who made it. It belongs to us, and so we can do with them as we choose.

86 The Spectrum of Disciplines

Putting works of people under the control of an intermediary, such as with a teacher in a Modernist class eager to show us how to understand it, destroys this immediacy. The class itself turns the work into a stone: it's required and part of the curriculum. The Modernist university encourages, indeed requires, intermediaries (professors) to grab the tiller and steer, hard and decisively, whereas the artistic integrity of the work is best served by no hand at all on the tiller, or only in case of imminent crash.

I experienced what happens when the crash is not avoided in a seminar between US Naval Academy students and St. John's College students where a Johnnie, as they are called, confused the lover and the beloved in Plato's *Phaedrus* and was going full speed ahead with an argument that was simply wrong. A Naval Academy professor tried to correct the student, but was slapped down by the St. John's tutor, who insisted that the student should be able to continue uncorrected. And the student did, thereby wasting a good bit of the limited time allotted to the seminar. Total lack of control is as bad as too-tight control. But at most institutions, the latter is the greater danger, especially from eager Assistant Professors itching to show off their graduate school learning and apply their dissertations or their upcoming article, and to set themselves up for a favorable tenure decision.

The center of the college and university is the experience of students, not the "research" that professors in the humanities and social sciences are so proud of generating. Yet many of these are relieved when finally the pressure is off to produce these things nobody knows what to do with—if not with a favorable tenure decision (increasingly rare these days), then retirement. This skew of priorities got more intense as the Modernist century wore on: in the 1950s no PhD degree was required to become a college teacher. Now it is necessary to hold one in hand, or have its awarding be a done deal, even to apply for a job as Assistant Professor (not that there are many such jobs available).

In the middle area of the scale, there is overlap between what during the Modernist era came to be seen as separate disciplines, and the most interesting people tend to be those who take in material from many different kinds of sources. Great novelists know a lot about human psychology without ever having taken a college course. The arts incorporate cultural facts about the world in which they came to be—sometimes in reverse image, the way the escapist Hollywood films of the 1930s with Fred and Ginger in ballrooms were an alternative to the grim reality of the Depression. Or they show gender and racial relationships of their world. Yet these are aspects, not the individual work. Works are primarily stand-alone objects, and far too often in college literature classes the individual work disappears and what is taught is second-rate sociology or psychology, or taken as an example of literary theory, which is almost always second-rate philosophy. Or: Food in Jane Austen? Sanitation in Dickens? If you want to do history, do history. Don't try to make it artsy by hooking on to a novelist.

Notes

1 Rawls, *A Theory of Justice*.
2 Sagan, *The Demon-Haunted World*.
3 Weber, "The Scholar's Work," and in numerous other essays concerning bureaucracies. For example, *Economy and Society*.
4 Weber, "The 'Objectivity' of Knowledge."

11

FUNDAMENTAL RULES

The reality of lived life is so variable moment to moment that it seems reasonable that people would look for a finite number of basic rules we follow all the time, such as the way Northrop Frye laid down the basic patterns of all literature, or Lévi-Straus of societies with his dualities.[1] (What allows me to judge this impulse as "reasonable"? That sounds like an objective judgment. But I could also say "I see that," which sounds like a completely subjective assertion.) Once we learn these rules, it seems, the rest is just details. But the urge to find basic rules that human beings follow whether they know it or not, whether they set out to do so or not, is not itself a given, and creates several problems. These rules are usually the province of philosophy.

I hated Kant in college, the Kant of the *Critique of Pure Reason*. How dare he tell me what the givens of being human were? He's a human, I'm a human. I can argue that Kant is wrong, because what he says is by definition precise and so is in the world rather than standing outside it giving its workings. Something allows me to make this argument, something larger than both of us. You never conceptualize the whole world or give Most Fundamental Rules, because when you do you place them back in the world.

Now I am typing: I am not perceiving in time and space. Yes, you are, says Kant: you reach out to the keyboard and follow the letters as they form words and sentences on the page. If that isn't time and space, I don't know what is. But time and space are far from my mind, I object. I am listening to the spirits within me (?) that tell me what sentence to write so I write the right one. Descartes would say, that's not what I'm conscious of.

Dummy, says Kant, I'm talking about what's behind consciousness: consciousness has qualities that produce our world. But you got to behind consciousness through your consciousness, I object. No, says Kant. I got there through reason. I ask, what allows you to reason about time and space being the structure of

DOI: 10.4324/9781003217688-14

consciousness? Is that reasoning in time and space? No, says Kant. It is logically before all that.

Immanuel, I say, you are just the Enlightenment version of Scholastic philosophy perplexed by having to answer whether God is in the time and space He created. If we say God created the world, it seems there was a time when time (?) was not. Why does God change to introduce time and the world? *Can* God change? For the Middle Ages, the attempt to get behind what is was expressed in divine terms. For the Enlightenment, it was expressed in terms of Reason: transcendental/metaphysical/synthetic a priori, etc. Same attempt, same result. When we make words, they are precise, and precise words become things in the world, not beyond it. And if Kant wants to say, Yes! Things in time and space!, then just let him. There's no end to this game of "I get behind you so you get behind me so I get behind you…" It's all individuals doing it. The only way people can get beyond people is by using, as counters, entities that are not human: the atoms, microbes, and astral bodies of science.

My talking of the "cloud" (more on this below) is an attempt to be as vague as possible, like refusing to see God as an old man with a white beard on a golden throne, a sort of Unitarian view of God, indistinguishable from the Earth Spirit. It's vague with respect to available alternatives we are familiar with. But it's not completely vague, and inevitably someone will come along who tries to get beyond this. That fact is not a failure of my reasoning (not a "schoolboy howler" or something equally condescending), it's an essential part of my point. Everything we say or do is part of its context. We know that in an exchange like "Will it rain today?" / "I don't know, let me look on my phone" / "OK, I'm waiting" / "It says 100% chance at noon," we don't have to explain rain, or today, or phone, or I.

But with an essay like this one, I don't know the reader; you don't know me; we're not next to each other, and we aren't talking about the same day when we talk about rain—or maybe not about the same conception of Kant when we talk about Kant. Besides, I dumped this problem in your lap and am proposing a solution. Maybe you don't see as a problem what I see as a problem. Maybe you don't agree that I have made it go away. Maybe you see the problem but think it trivial. Of course, maybe, just maybe, it's a problem that you were somehow worried by without having the words to articulate it and it feels to you as if you found someone speaking to your deepest convictions. (I felt that way when I read Wittgenstein's *Tractatus* in college.) So it's not clear whether you will enter into either the posing of the problem or the solution. Works like this, in order to be even as independent of situations as they are—which they have to be to some degree to be portable from one situation to another—provide both parts of what are usually divided up among people, the question and the response. This means they are opaque to most people without someone to break these apart again. And that's what a skilled teacher can do. There is a point to education, if done right.

The problem with religions, all of which at least gesture at what allow us to do all that we do, is the same as the problem with articulating rules of being human using Reason. Namely, that each conception of what lies beyond the everyday

90 The Spectrum of Disciplines

world that formalizes into a set of beliefs or actions has to express this act of running behind ourselves in precise terms in the world. Religion invariably develops concrete form. For Christianity, it's the Holy Trinity and the Virgin Birth, plus Jesus rising from the dead; the words of the Qur'an for Islam; the countless precise rules of Leviticus for orthodox Judaism, the various forms of the Hindu gods and their geographical connection to the Indian subcontinent for Hinduism, and so on. And this leads to problems when one such concretization of what cannot be made concrete conflicts with another.

There is nothing intrinsic about this conflict; people create it or not. My gesture at the Beyond is the only acceptable one! No, mine! No, mine! Minorities can insist that everybody be like them, as can majorities, or each of two equal factions. There are, to be sure, religions that resist making the Beyond concrete, such as Unitarianism, or Hinayana Buddhism, or Quakerism, but these are small sects indeed. Concrete visualization and/or a clear list of dogmas seem to work better for most people, perhaps because they have a daily life they have to attend to, so that religion is easier if it becomes once again merely things in the world rather than a gesture outside it. Just tell me what to sign off on so I can go on with my life!

So can we never get abstract on humans? Of course we can—but only under precise circumstances, which may or may not be replicated again or elsewhere. People make these abstractions about humans for specific reasons in a particular set of circumstances; something close to these precise reasons has to occur again for them to be useful or relevant. And we always have to determine that this is so. Those who made these abstractions will likely insist that their abstractions are always in any case true or the case, but this is the same sort of statement as saying that God is an old man with a white beard: we accept this or not for personal reasons. (This is the paradox of the scale: the more abstract the assertion regarding humans and their situation in the world, the more personal is their acceptance.)

We can't assume that abstractions are applicable just because we hear them or they are written down. They might be, but we always have to judge this. For example: following Kant, Hannah Arendt asserts confidently that there are three basic mental functions: thinking, willing, and judging.[2] Only three? And separate? I am driving on I-95 back to Annapolis from Philadelphia. I am looking at other cars so as not to have an accident. I want to get home: willing? I am reflecting on the speed and license plates of other cars: thinking? I am calculating the speeds of other cars. Are they going to cut in? Is this judging? How can Arendt be so sure there are only three functions, and that they are separate? If the assertion is that this is always true whether or not I agree, then this is as "meaningless" (to borrow a term from the positivists) as a statement about God or the afterlife.

The first problem with making quasi-scientific assertions about the middle of the scale is that the rules apparently don't prohibit their violation. Someone can be guilty of a false syllogism, say—like Woody Allen's joking "All men are mortal, Socrates is a man, therefore all men are Socrates."[3] Or people may well disagree about whether the apparent causality is strong enough to conclude real causality. Yes, I know she hates X, but the fact that she avoided X could have been caused by something else—sure, could have, but where is the evidence of this—here, right here—doesn't seem strong enough to me... Juries or panels of judges simply vote, and philosophy professors love examples with no clear answer so they can talk about the larger issues. (The over-cited "trolley problem" that purposely tries to get us to weigh the relative importance of two unrelated things, our actions and their effects, is a good example of a problem that can generate endless discussion and never be solved.[4]) And we don't say, You've violated the rule of causality; we say, You haven't proven your assertion. Rules turn out to be irrelevant to actions.

What allows a judge to say that the assertions of the plaintiff have not been convincing? What if you disagree? There's a system to disagree—up to a certain point. In the USA, that point is the votes of the Supreme Court—and four people can disagree, to no effect, with five. It all comes down to individuals voting. Using their judgment? Maybe also their political orientation (what is this?) and their perceptions (what are these?). Fact is, a five–four vote decides the issue.

Professors are rather like judges. What allows me to write on a freshman paper that the writer has failed to substantiate the paper's thesis? It's not an appeal to fundamental laws, unless the assertion is that I do so whether or not I am doing so—which is a power play. After all, the writer clearly thought that what was written was good enough. For that person, it may have been, perhaps because the writer was used to talking to people who shared the same bottom line. For the writer, the conclusion is reached, but perhaps not for others. I know about the others, which apparently the writer doesn't. Once it's committed to paper and set out in the world, it may encounter these other kinds of people. That's a fact I know and the writer apparently doesn't, or thinks unimportant. It's not an appeal to fundamental laws. So the second problem is that the more fundamental the law, the less relevant it is to life. We don't actually appeal to such laws, and they never stopped anybody from violating them.

The third major problem is therefore that the deeper they are buried, which is to say the more fundamental they are held to be, the stronger the case for finding them irrelevant. It's difficult to actually disagree with them, as in saying (for example) that no, we don't conceive in terms of time and space, because it would take work to say how else we do conceive. Worse, we'd have to accept the terms laid out by this initial assertion of offering something else of the same sort. We can't disagree with Kant by offering him a peanut butter sandwich: we would have to play his game. But in fact this isn't a given; we can take an entirely different tack—say, by saying that sure, we need to think in order to think about something that isn't thinking (time/space/causality, etc. are things ascribed to the world, only Kant's point is we put them there), but that is the problem of concluding that the fact that we look through a window means everything is most fundamentally Something Seen Through a Window. Or that everything we see in the morning is most fundamentally morning-lit, not the things revealed by morning. Says who? Each of these is a particular emphasis for particular reasons. And we can simply apply other emphases.

But the priestly caste knows how to protect itself. If anyone says, just read the novel!, the disdainful response from literature professors is that this is intellectually

92 The Spectrum of Disciplines

jejune: "naïve" realism which we all know (sniff) to be insufficient. No, we don't all know it to be insufficient, and it's not just people beneath notice who just interact with the world—everybody does outside of the classroom, for starters.

The disadvantage of no talk in a forum that presupposes talk is that it seems like an admission of impotence. Talk is king in Modernist academia, an endless flow of talk. Listening to professors explain endlessly that they are necessary to explain how inaccessible the world is (so why listen? If it's inaccessible it's inaccessible), how facts are only "facts" and how works are about other works, is like being caught in a stuck elevator with a hyperactive motormouth. What they are saying may make sense and we may be willing to consider it if it is written down and read slowly with a glass of wine where we can stop reading at will, but under the circumstances of having to listen, it's just annoying. And we can't separate out words from their circumstances—or at least, we get a false sense of them if we do.

That's the failure of one of the primary precursors of the Modernist worldview: Freud insisted that a patient assent right then and there to what Dr. F is telling (usually) her. It's the coercion of the situation we resist, and the power relation it creates. That's why arguments generally don't change minds: the person has to want to hear the other point of view, and be in control of taking it in. Academics is a situation of control of the student by the professor. Conversely, the poetic power of Freudian ideas continues to resonate because we can read them and let them seep in gradually, as well as accepting whatever percentage of them and at whatever level of generality seem attractive to us. Freudian concepts are best taken in generalized and diluted form: how much poorer would we be without the reminder that what we think we are doing isn't what we later admit (or that others now see) we were doing, that we criticize others for our own unadmitted faults, and that things we think we have gotten over continue to determine our behavior. All these things work as generalizations about some people some of the time in the area between personal preferences and science. It's when they are pushed to the level of abstract assertions about the structure of all people (beware of the word "structure")—or this or that technical term held to be in all people—that they over-reach. As a poet, Freud is marvelous. As a scientist, he is silly and annoying. We can say something similar about Wittgenstein: as a poet, fabulous. Content, not so much.

We accept the focus of the lens that we accept. Kant was following Descartes's lead in making the thinker primary, but this itself can be opposed: all conceptions of the world rest on unarticulated presuppositions, which someone can subsequently articulate and challenge. In seeking the Most Fundamental Rules of Human Whatever (thought, perception, apperception) we always lay the groundwork for something else, including the opposite, to be articulated.

Let's say that a point of view seems plausible. There's nothing clearly wrong with it, given its unarticulated presuppositions. The fact that it seems plausible for reasons we can't articulate means that someone can later articulate and then question these presuppositions, and disagree. Some things that are implausible are pretty commonly agreed to be so. Even if they don't seem implausible to us, they will be

Fundamental Rules **93**

shot down immediately as soon as we articulate them. Others survive longer—sometimes much longer.

Try being a professor to read and hear many student assertions that aren't plausible, but these screwups don't make it out of the classroom, and a philosophy that finds adherents and stays around for a while is a much stronger case: we shouldn't confuse the thinkers taught in a philosophy course with the arguments made now by human beings, any more than the paintings in the National Gallery in any country are representative of the paintings produced in that country. (That's the point of the adherents of a POV that is "underrepresented" by the mainstream. Only, someone having a different skin color isn't a reason for assuming that that person has a new argument or one worth considering.) Hundreds, perhaps thousands of reasonings are easily batted down and never survive for every one that is more difficult to kill, and does survive to make it to the syllabus.

Still, each clear position, even of a Great Thinker, draws a line that makes it easy for others to diverge from that line. In this sense, each philosophy, for this is what we call Most Fundamental Laws/Rules/Practices of humans, lays the groundwork for its own—what?—not disproof, not rejection, but of its own being cut down to size by another philosophy. Philosophers don't disprove predecessors, they just turn aside. The result is that philosophy should be seen cumulatively, not as a series of individuals, each of whom tries to map the whole. Instead, each new philosophy joins the list of possible problems to focus on. Does this problem seem yours? Then by all means read this philosopher. No? Then not.

For example: is Bishop Berkeley's idealism true? A lot of people had to admit he had a point (based on what laws, hmmm?). Sure, in a sense we do cause things to come to be in the act of our perceiving them. Shut your eyes, the world disappears. Only this requires, as in Descartes, the logical (meaning what?) Janus face to this extreme subjectivity, namely the extreme objectivity of God. And it completely leaves out the social world of other people who might well say, Hey! You didn't cause me to come to be! I was here all the time! And what of the defenders of objects who say, Hey! Why did the bowl of water you caused to be three days ago and then again today by perceiving it now have a lower level of water? Of course, I may have caused it to come to be with a lower water level but how did I know how to do that? And how much lower? It seems sensible to say it was there all the time, evaporating.

But what means sensible? It's just too much trouble to have the world consist only of God and me. Berkeley isn't true or false, or rather both—it is a specific focus that includes certain situations and shuts out others. But when the world consists of God and me, and I'm just going about my business, rather than drowning like the nuns of the *Deutschland*, Berkeley seems our man. Berkeley takes a small part of human existence and expands it to everything, as if valid for everyone all the time. This works for a time, perhaps, but its deficiencies soon become clear. So why not just give up trying to articulate Most Fundamental Laws of Being Human? We don't need them, being human. What we need Most Fundamental Laws for is the *not* Human, which we call the objective world—and we call the search for them, which is ongoing, science.

94 The Spectrum of Disciplines

Science abstracts from the world, and this is the basis of whatever degree of certainty it manages to achieve. So the world can always provide uncertain things that call the abstractions into question—and ultimately, with enough of these, disprove them. It's just that if we look in all the obvious places readily accessible to us for contrary evidence and don't find it, it will take something major for new evidence from new places using new methods to appear. So we call these scientific truths proven—based on the evidence we have, that is. And we are by definition ignorant of the other evidence that we don't have, and in fact may not exist. We can't always assume that a Bogeyman will pounce on us from the darkness—usually there is nothing there. But if a Bogeyman does pounce, it will be from the darkness, because otherwise we'd see him. Unless, of course, we are blind, or blinded, or unaware. Popper isn't wrong that all scientific conclusions are disprovable, but of course this doesn't mean that all are tottering—some are quite secure. Most Fundamental Structures in science are what science is about. This system works because it is not amenable to the objections of individuals—only to disproof, which is to say, actions in its own terms.

However, Most Fundamental Structures in the humanities and social sciences, such as philosophy or literary theory (or ham-fisted social analyses like Marx's)—rather than clarifications of particular problems—always fail to deliver on their lure. This is so not only because they turn out to be too general to help with specific human issues, but also because by articulating them we place them in the world as precise entities. And that makes them specific, things *in* the world (and hence limited), rather than underlying it. And so we are able, with time, to show their irrelevance and deficiencies, the limitations all specific things have built into them merely because they are specific things in the world, not beyond it.

Moreover, the longer we hear about them, the more tired we grow of them: all these things are things done by people, and people crave novelty. We can never Understand people for all time, just understand (small u) specific aspects of specific people for the present and perhaps a bit more. We are (perhaps) interested in precise ways of looking at people for a while, and then we aren't. And that's where we are with Modernism. As all totalitarian rulers who repeat their mantras over and over discover, people get tired of hearing these, and become increasingly aware of their divergence from the truth.

Take the common assertion from the middle of the scale (psychology? sociology?) that all men want to spread their seed and so are naturally sexually promiscuous. I'd say I'm a man. But what if I am monogamous? Or horrified at the thought of spreading my seed? Am I then not a man? Men are chauvinistic, or assertive, say. Are these generalizations from experience? If so, how general? Does the conclusion refer only to the group studied? Was it studied correctly? This is the inexhaustible back and forth flow of the middle of the scale that is in constant flux. It is clearly part of the agon of life rather than something outside of it, as it has been conceived of being in the Modernist era. We are all the time making generalizations about our family members, people in our town, work colleagues, and various other groups of individuals in the world (novels, paintings, restaurants, fashions, pets, etc., etc., etc.) that we gradually confirm or chip away at, or first one then the other, before turning to other generalizations we are building or tearing down.

The academic disciplines that Modernism created, those in the middle of the scale, simply took larger bites of the world than those we take as individuals: not just the men we know but all men, not just our office colleagues but office structures in general, not just people who look and act different and who maybe live in far-away places and maybe have different-colored skin but different societies or cultures or races, and so on; not just the novels we have read but all texts, not just the words we use but all language, and so on: sociology, anthropology, psychology, gender studies, literary theory, linguistic philosophy, and so on were born. Yet now these huge bites have gotten smaller and smaller and the divisions that allowed us to take these huge bites less and less tenable. We no longer believe in societies or races or genders or literature (or national literatures: goodbye comparative literature). Anything anybody does is grist for the academic McMill. Academic disciplines in the middle of the scale have blurred and fragmented to the point where they are almost indistinguishable from each other and from what we do everyday in the world.

We all make abstractions, but we do so at our peril. There is always a gulf between abstract and particular that has to be bridged: maybe this abstraction captures something about me, but by definition it doesn't capture everything, because it's an abstraction. A map shows the shape of a single field, a county, a country, or a continent, but even the most precise map doesn't show everything. In any case, it is only visual. Where are the sounds, smells, feelings, associations we may have with these places? They have fallen victim to the abstraction. Abstraction gives us the false sense of greater power: our purview covers such a large territory! But this means of necessity that we fail to see the particulars. What does a map of Italy, or even Rome, have to do with sitting in a café in front of the Pantheon sitting our cappuccino? Maps can save us from crashing into rocks, or tell us what road to take, or where to land our soldiers. But these are specific uses; maps are things in the world, not outside of it.

We are reminded of Yertle the Turtle in Dr. Seuss's eponymous book-fable: Yertle declared himself the lord of all he saw. But what effect did that have on the trees he saw, or the cow? And of course he was brought down by not considering the conditions of this broad but not deep view: a turtle named Zak (to rhyme with "stack," as in stack of the turtles that Yertle uses as a throne), who burps and topples Yertle, now without his surveying power, into the mud. Adopting the point of view of the abstract doesn't give us more knowledge; it just takes us away from the particular. And Yertle, like professors of the humanities and social sciences, forgot the very real conditions that underlay his wider view, which he mistook for control. The reality is that the wider your view, the less you control—if the focus is on your view. Science doesn't emphasize the view, or the human relation of control. It's about abstractions, not individuals.

We don't actually need fundamental truths about people to function as people, because we're already people. And we didn't make ourselves people. What we do

96 The Spectrum of Disciplines

is what we do. Of course, this doesn't mean specific things we do, like errors or emphases or new usages and actions. Thinking that we can't be wrong with language usage was the problem with Stephen Pinker's view of language.[5] He thought there is no such thing as a grammatical error—people talk the way birds make nests. But a grammatical error is possible, as it's possible for a bird to use too much shredded newspaper in its nest and find it soggy. Error is less fundamental than the fact of language itself. Of course, there are degrees of mastery and sophistication of language. Pinker clearly did not correct freshmen papers, which are full of all sorts of errors. Says who? I do, and I'm the one correcting them. Cooking is human too, but we can still burn the roast.

But of course we can make statements about things, not people. And for all of this we need to invent new words. We are not stars, or blood corpuscles, or DNA, or bugs, so of course these statements are possible. This is what we mean by science. It's quite true that we are making the statements about things not us, and we can consider this fact—say, by pointing out that we have personal investment in certain sorts of statements, or turn to them under certain circumstances. But just as we say that we see something—not just a subjective sense-impression—and we *can* say this (though we can see everything as only our subjective sense impressions), we can say that the world outside us exists.

Just as it is true that paintings are squares on canvas (or some close variation), or all statements with words (as opposed to gestures or grimaces) are in language, so it's quite true that everything perceived is what we perceive: we can certainly make this fact primary. Similarly, we can make primary that everything in France is French. Or, alternatively, we can see not French birds but birds, not French sand but sand, not French enthusiasm but enthusiasm—and can also make distinctions between things we should see as more French than others. Modernism saw the medium as primary in everything—but other foci do not. There is no way to decide between seeing everything as a perception of me and seeing me in a world outside of me—these are both possible, just as it's possible to focus either on the windowpanes, or on what we see through them. Of course science is possible! That doesn't mean we can't be wrong—the sun might not rise tomorrow if the sun explodes, for example.

Philosophy doesn't even have to be false, just have its limitations made clearer by too great generalization and repetition. Take Cartesian doubt again. By making doubt central, Descartes makes clear that most of the time we don't doubt, so doubt can't be fundamental, and universalizing it is arbitrary, not to mention somewhat bizarre. Doubt is a specific action, and the generalization of a specific set of circumstances to everything misunderstands reality—which is essentially what Descartes concludes by saying that God looks after us. His bottom line is that sometimes we doubt but usually we don't, so it's a deformation of reality to make this central. That's true, and that's what we all know. Or how about thinking? Do we always think? Do we cease to exist when we don't? Why try to universalize something we know to be specific? Sometimes we cook dinner, but does that mean that's the central act of our lives? For some people, perhaps. But most of us aren't chefs. It makes more sense to write a cookbook so others can pick it up when they are focused on this one action, not assert that this is central.

Philosophy itself is therefore intrinsically misleading. Philosophy picks one question to focus on, or a small number, out of the infinity of things we could be considering, and the fact of attention makes this central. We have to figure out whether we should doubt our senses! We have to decide when life begins in the individual person! We have to know whether there was time before God created the world! We have to know whether angels have male/female gender! We have to be able to say what constitutes ethical behavior! We have to know whether we can access other minds! We have to know whether science is possible! We have to know what the nature of Justice is!

In fact, before these questions became, for their time and circumstances, central, people still ate, slept, carried on, and thought about possibly all other things than this particular question. And that proves we don't actually need to think about these things, or answer the question. We think we do, but we don't. Besides, more or less abstract is a specific choice or place on the scale at a specific moment for specific purpose. Kant still ate and slept and took his walk (every day at the same time) while he was figuring things out to his satisfaction—and the world went on before he did so, nor was it changed after. Chomsky still said please and thank you to the grocery clerk (we hope) while he was meditating on the fundamental structure of all language (which we don't need in order to use words). More abstract gets both broader and weaker, like a skin stretched ever thinner over an ever larger area. What makes it break? Our saying heck with it, it's unrelated to what I actually do.

Perhaps a better analogy is that it's something buried so deep we don't see it on the surface any more. It might seem we are getting to the most fundamental aspects, but in fact we are simply getting further from what we need. Greater depth means we walk over it without knowing it's there. You don't have to be a pragmatist to note that if you never have to consider these things, they might as well not be there, because these are things about humans as people, not the inhuman entities of science.

Is the argument that there are no such things as "humans as people"? This is the argument of the brain-not-mind people. I say: I'm a person and I refuse to accept this because I am its living disproof. Go ahead, tell me I'm a machine and not a person rejecting this assertion. Fine; I'm (meaning unclear) still rejecting it. See the impasse? And by the way, you're a person too, though you are arguing that there is no such thing as people who are in any way different than machines. You play leapfrog over me, but then I play leapfrog over you, ad infinitum.

Wittgenstein, who shared my sense of the transitory and exasperating nature of this process, concluded too harshly that such questions shouldn't be asked at all. But clearly these questions were central for the people who asked them. This is a collective version of the way relatively small things (small at least in the before and after phases) take over our attention: we may be obsessed (as we say) with a person for sexual reasons, or to vent our fury and exact revenge—think Ahab and Moby

98 The Spectrum of Disciplines

Dick—or with a new object we covet, or the leaves falling from our neighbor's tree onto our property.

We realize that we have to put these aside for some things—getting dinner, concentrating on the road, watching the kids. And we can re-focus or concentrate, as we say. Those who can't, who for example are unable to listen to a teacher because all they can think about is how the pencil on their desk should be pointing one way and not the other, are diagnosed as abnormal. So most people are not completely the prisoners of their obsessions. Still, if we have a leisure moment and we think yet again of person X or Y, or of something we absolutely have to solve, or if that is in fact our work (nobody would want to take the obsessions from a scientist or a composer), we allow these to take us over. It's not at all like the stream of consciousness of the Modernists, it's like being turned into someone else, the borders between us and the world dissolved, become this idea—or Emerson's giant eye.

What determines our conviction that we need X or Y? Advertising, perhaps. Or following what we call a train of thought—that can be interrupted by random ideas popping up. I am paying attention to what I am writing here, but I confess it was interrupted multiple times for me to check my email, or the time, or to look up the Cantonese proclivity to eat wild animals. Some things central to our attention are made central by others, some are ours alone. This is also true of ideas that are general enough to figure in the history of ideas (and who says more general ideas are more valuable than fashion or toy choices?). They occupy center stage as long as they do, and then don't. We can get over a crush on a hot girl or boy, or wonder, when the fire burns out, why we absolutely had to have that suit, hand-bag, or car, or why we went through a Gertrude Stein phase.

Most Fundamental Structures about humans also don't pre-empt conflict or disagreement, which is usually the point of insisting on them. If you say everybody is conceiving in terms of time and space, then so are the people disagreeing with you saying they aren't doing it. And saying they can't say this because that's an impossibility presupposes your position. Most people won't disagree because they don't care, which is the ultimate rejection.

The logic for Most Fundamental Rules about humans is like that of the onto-logical proof of the existence of God. This fails because we are conceiving of God in worldly terms, as having qualities, and so can't conclude that a trans-worldly entity that nonetheless has worldly qualities (such as existence) exists. Maybe God has an alternative to either existence or non-existence in our worldly sense? We can't prove the existence of God, but we can postulate God the way we can pos-tulate an objective world. Only, we can say things about the objective world, because it is unlike us only in not being human. That leaves a lot of qualities we can ascribe to it.

Science doesn't offer rules. It offers facts. Rules are only with respect to humans, and only in the center of the spectrum. Facts only apply to inhuman scientific entities, not people as individuals or in groups, assuming these groups are com-posed of individuals. This is so not for metaphysical reasons, for example the

Fundamental Rules   99

existence of something we call human free will, but because individuals can never generate general facts valid for all—this is Hume's point about the futility of trying to get science out of a series of individual perceptions. The logical positivists focused on this distinction by insisting that "is" did not imply "should." It doesn't—which is why science and morality are at different places on the spectrum.

The center of the spectrum is intrinsically shot through with problems because it consists of people generalizing (at the more personal end) and abstracting (as it approaches the science end) about people. This cuts out the particularities of individuals and their lives, and that seems a big saving of time and attention. But because we are particular people, generalizations will always be transitory until revised and/or approximate. And we don't need to appeal to abstractions to help us with our lives when things are going as expected (and we learn what is expected, and can revise this)—just when they aren't. The more inevitable we claim these abstractions are, the less they actually matter to us, because inevitable is inevitable, and we can't appeal to them to solve problems. Neither do the too granular studies trying to conclude that people are more X or Y if their reaction time to an image of a certain sort is 0.2 seconds faster or slower than others. These laboratory facts nowadays are rarely used to help us solve problems outside the laboratory, just to amass factoids that go no further than the experiment itself: this image, this reaction time in these subjects. Thus the world of their applicability is confined to scholarly journals or the classroom. Do we seriously believe that people being people need research into people to be people? Abstractions are useful only in solving particular problems within the act of being a person, not the act itself.

Abstractions about people towards the science end of the scale are justified by likening them to science, which generally consists of countless small discoveries and increments. But the increments of science add up to something outside themselves because they put tiny pieces in the puzzle of the objective world, which is to say the world outside of individual people. We have to be sure we create these increments correctly—no contamination, no bias, double blind, etc.—which is very hard to do and constantly subject to revision when we place the results of an experiment in the real world: just because Chemical X responded this way to Chemical Y in the laboratory (and can be shown to do so repeatedly) we can't say for sure how it will respond in the real world where X and Y are in larger contexts which may influence the outcome. The translation for science to reality is, to evoke Popper again (whose guiding conception was science as process rather than as result), never more than more probable—though this can get to a stage of so probable we don't know of any exceptions, which we may even call certainty. And we can always realize later that the translation to the real world is imperfect and try again.

But the pieces that science can put into the puzzle are all outside of people. We have no special access to knowledge about them and so we must collaborate with others using methods we agree on. We can have no dog in the fight: wishing cancer or nebulae were different than they are cuts no mustard. That's not true for science-miming experiments in the middle of the spectrum that aim at conclusions

100 The Spectrum of Disciplines

about people. Because we are inside our (so to say) peoplehood, we have a privileged perspective on people, intrinsically have a dog in the fight. Any scientific statements about us as individual people (as opposed to our spinal cords or our response to medicines X or Y or the effects on us of global warming) are subject to our review and consideration and possible alteration or even rejection.

This can't be merely because we don't like them, the way we don't like (say) pistachio ice cream, because these statements are further along the spectrum toward science than statements about ice cream. But we can say that the fact that subjects respond in certain ways to the laboratory does not imply what it's held to imply—for example that they are showing the human/male/racial/national capacity for compassion or aggression or racism. We can disagree with the conclusion, but we have to express this in the same quasi-scientific terms in which it was expressed: the data do not justify this conclusion because X or Y. But the difference between assertions in the middle of the scale from science is that though we have to justify our response, we can start from a personal angle as we cannot do with asteroids or bacteria—or if we do, we show that we do not understand what science is. (This is true of some people even today, and was true of many more in the nineteenth century, as the Darwin debate shows.)

Science warns against its practitioners assuming that correlation means causality, which indicates that this is an eternal problem for science, what has to be avoided over and over (and sometimes isn't). However, this jump is the very basis of the social sciences and humanities, the source of their eternal hope and eternal disappointment. The discovery that (say) a certain percentage of self-identified gay men in a sample had an enlarged X or a smaller Y than self-identified straight men can't lead to the conclusion that someone with such a condition will be gay. Or can it? First, we have the purely scientific problems: sample size and nature, confirmation bias, treatment of data etc. Then same goes for genes: Maybe if you have a certain gene you will possibly? certainly? get disease X or Y—that's the scientific part. But usually that's all we know. When? How bad will the disease be? What will you feel or think about it? Science is very narrow. The problems come from re-inserting it into the wide world.

That wide world includes all sorts of oh-so-human factors. Any (say) genetic or scientific correlation that results in the suggestion that one group—say women or non-whites—are in any way inferior will, in today's political climate, be both attacked as science and prevented from yielding consequences. Or we can grant the science but still deflect its consequences in the world. For example, it is true that on average women have less upper body strength than men. So what do we do with this? That's what's up to individuals. We can (a) attack the division male/female, as for example women with high testosterone levels or chromosomal abnormalities; (b) grant the distinction but point out that there are outliers in each group, strong women and weak men, so we can't (say) forbid women to do jobs that typically require upper body strength; and (c) address a further problem: if there is only one woman in a group of men, do we need to ensure other women there to give her company?—this argument has been used to justify gender and racial affirmative action—which means not using the initial criterion as rigorously or at all but making the makeup of the group its own end.

If science tells us that cavemen got fat during fat years or seasons to guard against lean, like hibernating bears, does this mean it's OK to be obese nowadays? What exactly is the connection between cavemen and us? If we put a number on human intelligence, this leads to results that some people reject: the rejection comes first, then a way must be found to block the path to this conclusion. Possibilities include attacking the idea that this number is scientific, accepting it but saying that it should not be considered for anything, or for some things that are specified, or relativizing it by saying it is only one relevant number (this is the idea behind the concept of "social IQ"). There is no limit to the obstacles people can and perhaps should throw in the way of moving from science to people. And we can do this because we are people. Science is outside individuals, but it's individuals doing it— and deciding how to apply it. Sure, it creates problems. But that's just the way things are. And how much more is all this true of things on the scale closer to the personal—what we call the humanities and social sciences.

Kant asked how the (objective) results of science are possible, rather than the real question, namely why (subjective) people do science. NB: Only people do science, and it doesn't do itself even given the fact that its results are statements about the world outside people. Because Kant started by separating objective from subjective, he was obliged to reinsert the subjective at a more fundamental level into the objective structure of The Way Things Are in order to reconnect them. But this has no power over the subjective and can't solve human problems, because it is a statement about the objective. If he was trying to convince science that it should accept the fact that people do it, he'd have had a better case. Convincing people that they are necessary to science so it's OK to do it doesn't take that many words because people are what do science, so nothing changes.

Occam's Razor alone should have made people cease reading *The Critique of Pure Reason* long ago. We don't need Most Fundamental Facts about people because there's nothing to fix about being people in general, just about specific problems of people. Structures held to be the Most Fundamental Structures of people are by definition irrelevant to people's daily life, and if they really are Most Fundamental, then they underlie everything including people rejecting them or ignoring them. And because we are people, we can continue being people without articulating them. And what does articulating prove anyway? Or what does it help? If they are necessary they are necessary, which means useless to us as individuals. Let's move on.

There's nothing wrong with being in vast area between science and personal preferences where the two are mixed in varying degrees, but the temptation should be resisted to use the inhuman as a substitute for the human, the general for the specific, saying "always works like this" rather than "seems to be the rule but who knows?" Ham-fisted operators in this realm like Marx know (or say they know) what individuals will do because they know what economic entities will do and individuals are never any more than the instantiation of the economic entity. The

102 The Spectrum of Disciplines

more subtle thinker Weber knew that no amount of social science could explain Raphael's paintings. How does my economic status explain the stance of this essay? Having time and health enough to write it is general, but why the particular argument? My being male? The particular argument, mind you, not its tenor or cast or whatever. Being white? (I think I'm white but have never been genetically tested—maybe I'm not, and what would that explain?) Being American? From Maryland? From its Eastern Shore? Being 189 cm tall? Liking Mozart and Vermeer?

The social sciences always skew toward the scientific away from the personal, otherwise they wouldn't be social *science* at all. Yet they are most successful when their claims are the least scientific, because generalizations about people can always have exceptions. If we say that being born as X or Y or under these or those circumstances means we *will* do or be A or B, we are likely to have our argument punctured by exceptions. Sure, not everyone born to a crackhead mother with a dozen half-siblings ends up badly. Most do, unfortunately. But that's where the personal sorts insist that, for example, we can always pull ourselves up by our own bootstraps. It's possible. So we need to pull back on our assertions and say we have correlation but not causality—and statistically speaking, our generalizations about the world (children of crackhead mothers with a dozen half-siblings don't usually graduate at the top of their class at the University of Chicago) are worthy of consideration.

Notes

1 Frye, *Anatomy of Criticism: Four Essays*. Levi-Strauss, *Structural Anthropology*.
2 Arendt, *The Life of the Mind*.
3 Woody Allen, as both writer of and character in the film *Love and Death*.
4 Trolley problem. Much discussed but perhaps best summarized: en.wikipedia.org/wiki/Trolley_problem.
5 Pinker, *The Language Instinct*.

12

VERIFIABILITY

Things at the personal end of the spectrum, if they require more information (is the cat in?), can usually be dealt with by the individual using normal perceptual tools. Are the keys on the table? Yes. Or: I don't know but I'll look. Or: I can't say because I'm not at home. The logical positivists were obsessed with things at this end of the spectrum because they seemed to be things we could settle and move on. They called assertions here verifiable. The keys are on the table: we can verify, or so it seems. God is an old man with a white beard: not verifiable. The cat is in: verifiable. But: Beauty is the ultimate good? Not, it seems, verifiable.

However, this distinction is one of degree, and it is open to revision. Whether we say a question can be answered or not depends on what we know and what we believe to exist as possible sources of information. If any of this changes, and it can, the question changes position. Suddenly an experiment exists to find out X or Y; a librarian knows where to find a book that is exactly what you were looking for. So "verifiable" is not a quality of the statement, but instead a statement we make about our relationship with the world that can later be changed. We believe it to be something a person can find out. But we can be wrong, perhaps as a result of changing or misjudged circumstances. It is not the case that assertions about the physical world are verifiable and those about other realms are not. The causality is the opposite; we call what we take to be verifiable the physical world. To be sure, we don't have to know how to verify it to call it verifiable. An assertion about the universe that we as yet have no way to prove can still be held to be verifiable. But this is an assertion of faith. We don't see any reason it shouldn't be, some day. That's like saying that Disease X, say cancer, is in theory curable. We don't know whether it is or not—that's just our goal. What if we had said that of course we can at some point determine the position of electrons in an atom? Heisenberg says not. That itself can be a discovery. Hmmm; I guess we were wrong. So verifiable is based on what we know and believe, not a type of statement.

DOI: 10.4324/9781003217688-15

104 The Spectrum of Disciplines

If I say the cat is on the mat, it seems we can verify this. But what of an apparent assertion phrased as a question/expression of puzzlement? The gold standard seems to be: We're going to the store (firm assertion to a recalcitrant child, chopping motion with hand, frowning face). But this is only one place on quite a large spectrum of other things these words can function as. We're going to the store? (Incredulous—as in NOW? Throwing hands wide apart, bobbling head, raised eyebrows.) We're going to the store. (Softly, the implications just dawning on the speaker—maybe it means a good thing, maybe bad; head hanging, drooping body)... These seem to be assertions, but apparently aren't. In fact, there is no saying what these are—and usually we work on all parts of the spectrum. Nothing is gained by putting a label on one part and finding all else but one tiny fraction of them deficient. We know how to respond. If we don't, we ask for clarification. Are you serious or kidding? What are you referring to?

Most of us would agree that "my keys are on the table" is usually verifiable, shown to be true or false—by someone. We may not be home but we could call. Or maybe no one is home? We forgot our phone? Perhaps we believe we can check later. But here too we could be wrong. Perhaps the Berlin Wall went up while we were away and cut off our access to our house. So something that was verifiable yesterday suddenly becomes unverifiable today, at least by us or anybody we can think of. Saying "the keys are on the table" after the Wall has gone up and we know no way to get this information is no different from saying "the moon can sustain human life" in 1600 when we had no known way of finding this out. It moves further along the spectrum, becoming more difficult to confirm, bordering on impossible, which is also a fact of situations: we could in theory climb over the Wall, not get shot, go to our house, and so on. Once statements about the moon were unverifiable; now maybe they aren't. Even statements about God or heaven can in theory be verified—by dying. We just can't report back to the living. Or can we? Psychics claim we can.

The distinction between things we can do something about (as we say) and those we can't is one we re-negotiate constantly. Can we control grandpa? Our spouse? Our weight? Our impulses? The economy? What the Army is telling me to do? Finding out what we can control in our life and accepting that may be the key to calmness and serenity. A prisoner in a cell has more limited things under his control, but he has to find something he can control in order to stay sane—even if inside his head. That presumably was Sartre's intuition when he held that all people everywhere were free. Some have more evident constraints than others, we might object, but surely he was right that we accept what we can't choose if we cease to think about them as constraints.

Few of us feel constrained by having only two arms or having to walk rather than fly—though the sense that we are constrained can lead to great discoveries. The line between verifiable and not verifiable is a sub-set of changeable and not changeable, as all are statements that involve us and our position in the world. We make statements about the physical world outside us, but we're the ones making them, and so the possibility of alteration is built into the relationship. We (so to say) offload change onto ourselves by denying it to the physical world (which can have unchanging patterns of change). Chaos theory grew from the realization that these two apparently divergent realms of change and not-change are actually linked. Of course they are, just as a preference (today?) for chocolate over vanilla is on the same scale as statements about atoms. They're just not the same.

We can't verify statements about metaphysics or ethics, so Wittgenstein held them to lack meaning. And other thinkers who conflate verifiability with meaningfulness, as the logical positivists after Wittgenstein also did, insist that science is distinguished from religion or ethics by being verifiable like statements about the keys. But once again the distinction is something we make, which means the making is crucial, and the basis for the distinction is our belief that statements about the objective world are verifiable, even if not now or by us. We assign them to that category and call this the objective world. So sure, people make the objective world: by distinguishing it from the subjective. And the quality of this world is that it exists independently of us. We don't need sign-off on the objective world of science being totally independent of us, just more so than some things. We're alive in the world too, after all, so why would we think it's totally other than us? This is perhaps Goethe's intuition of a more holistic approach to a vital conception of nature. What we call the objective world is more or less separated from the subjective to the extent that we hold it to be so. If I am part of a living breathing nature, we are all one.

This way of proceeding may initially seem Hegelian: give me any contrast and I can relate the elements of the contrast. But my relation does not, unlike Hegel's, lead to a higher level of synthesis, merely to the fact that if the belt divides the upper torso from the lower, it also links them. The possibility of making a contrast means the contrasting elements are related, and that there is something linking the contrasting elements. The self doesn't alienate itself by talking in terms of a world outside it. During the period of the partition of Germany into East and West, the West (correctly) refused to acknowledge as a foreign country the Russian occupation zone that styled itself the German Democratic Republic, which the East repeatedly demanded it do. Thus the West installed in the East no "Embassy," *Botschaft*, but a *Ständige Vertretung*, a permanent representation. And East Germany was referred to by the West as the *inneres Ausland*, the near foreign. No realm that seems to exclude the human is further away than the near foreign, because we're the ones excluding it.

It's therefore backwards to say that an assertion is about the objective world if somebody (even if not us) can verify it. That's what makes it (in our view) objective. Nowadays we offload the responsibility for future verification on what we call "scientists," people who have that function. Most of us are not scientists, and even "scientists" is too wide a designation for the (say) half a dozen people worldwide who could possibly try to verify a specialized assertion. We don't ask to see the proofs of scientists; we just accept that they have been made. What about the assertions of priests that God is thus and so, or the assertion of philosophers that the Good is more X than the Beautiful? Plato thought we should just accept the

106 The Spectrum of Disciplines

assertions of people with greater insight than ourselves on such subjects, and religion is based on accepting the word without verification in the world of those more religiously enlightened.

It's not a quality of the statement itself that determines whether we express a view on it or not. If things are given to us on authority, we don't object they are meaningless—if we merely accept them. Paleontology is questioned by some religious sects, and far more students should question what they are told in English classes than do so. Religion wasn't questioned—until it was. "Show me" may work for everyday things in our personal lives, but (as Weber points out) those who arrived on the streetcar have no idea how it works.[1] We function quite well most of the time without being shown: this too is a specific demand, not a condition of carrying on.

The issue is whether we admit the possibility that others may simply see or understand more than ourselves. And this is a quality of individuals, not statements, one that may well be influenced by our particular circumstances. As children, we think that adults just know more and so take their word for things, but as adolescents most of us begin to question. If we are of a mind to hold that each person is as far-seeing as any other, as adults we will reject taking the word of people who purport to have access to realms we don't. We may even reject the idea of others having wisdom (accumulated experiences, not access to higher realms) we don't—and this is a factor of our own age as well as of other things: young adults full of beans typically reject the idea that the old, usually counseling caution, are wiser.

So it is quite true that a statement of the form of "God is Merciful" is unverifiable. But unverifiable doesn't mean meaningless if we don't ask for it to be verified—but accept it, say, because it comes from a priest. "Verifiable" turns out to be a fairly narrow criterion without any particular import. And a statement about nuclear physics for which we take scientists' word is only different from statements of ethics and metaphysics and religion (the bugbears of the positivists) to the extent we think it is. If we trust scientists the way we trust priests, the statements are similar. That is to simply abandon the focus on verifiability. And any focus can be abandoned or changed.

Assertions most evidently compose the scale that is defined by degrees of others' participation, which is undoubtedly why linguistic philosophy has been more interested in these than in other things we do and say (the definition is backwards: what falls on this scale involving others is most typically an assertion). Yet there is no absolute distinction between an assertion of fact—the gold standard of the logical positivists—and everything else. In any case, it's clear they didn't know what to do with anything that wasn't being offered for others to verify. That's the prejudice against the individual case, the personal, of all abstractions. Still, it's downright bizarre that language philosophers isolated one tiny part of the vast spectrum of language usage and proclaimed it primary—assertions of fact for which we allowed responses. We don't actually need science to live, as the Middle Ages demonstrated—but it certainly changes our lives if we do practice science, as the Modern Age demonstrates. However quasi-scientific consideration of everything does not change our lives—it just creates priestly castes whose primary goal is to preserve their status.

Many things we say and do are not on this scale at all. Oh really? / Hmmm. / I see. / Interesting. / Silence. "I see" can be "hmmm" or the opposite of "I don't get that," or it can be "you've made your point, now go on or shut up." All these are possible responses to any statement ranging from "We've discovered a new star!" to "I prefer vanilla." There are many events involving words that are not statements—though categorizing these doesn't determine what any individual thing is, it just gives sections of another spectrum that they may or may not fit in for however much time. Not only is not all language composed of assertions, but we don't always respond to assertions with judgments about truth and falsity. What to do with an assertion that is objected to not because it is true or false but because we have heard it too often from this person, or the tone of voice is grating? It isn't actually false, but we reject it all the same. What works best for the positivists was scientific assertions, because these are the most isolated from particular circumstances. But what about "Ben is a doofus." Who is Ben? Who says it? Under what circumstances? Is it serious? How much? Loving? How much? How is "doofus" understood by these people? Is this a term I use it all the time or is it new to me?

Problems arise with statements (only statements, not silence or things like Hmmm or Really? or Do you mean that? or Gracious!) that seem to combine aspects of different places of this scale—what look like statements not about people and are so abstract it seems other people should be able to vote on them, only we don't see how. Prime among these are statements of ethics and metaphysics that come from others. We may have no clue what the connection to the person is, so we can't respond. We also can't disagree with someone saying they are a Phillies fan, but we know it's the kind of thing we can't disagree with. (We can tell them they shouldn't be a Phillies fan, but we know we won't convince them.) This is undoubtedly why Wittgenstein concluded that some statements are meaningless. Is the Good more whatever than the Beautiful? We can make all sorts of Mad Libs sentences that no one would ever use as an assertion—the result might be like Lewis Carroll's "Jabberwocky" ("'twas brillig and the slithy toves," etc.) or Gertrude Stein, putting in nouns that don't belong or verbs or made-up versions of both but looking like things we understand (or for those hooked on abstractions, preserving the structure of the sentence). So in that sense, the assertion about the Good and the Beautiful is far from alone in being "meaningless."

But Stein and Dodgson/Carroll were doing what they did for other reasons than assertion. So what they are doing isn't meaningless, it just isn't what you think it is if you think it's like me saying to the family, "I made chicken for dinner." Did I or not? Probably I did. Why would I kid about that? But I might—say if it had become a joke how often I fixed chicken for dinner. But how about "I might consider cutting you some slack if I think about it." Proof/disproof? Even a statement that seems provable like "The cat is on the mat" is more probably an example in a textbook of philosophy or part of a lesson in poetry to first graders than something that would send us looking for the cat—if there is one at all.

108 The Spectrum of Disciplines

So merely because we don't see where to put an expression on the scale, we can't conclude the statement is "meaningless"—which is only a flaw in a small proportion of utterances anyway. Sometimes Hmmm means Hmmm, and pulling on your ear lobe means pulling on your ear lobe, as Sam Spade (Humphrey Bogart) in "The Big Sleep" notes. Somebody said that 'twas brillig—it's nonsense, sure, but that's the point. We don't throw it out. Even Gertrude Stein's works must have a point, we feel, and countless Assistant Professors have set about explaining them to you. What is meaningless to you may have meaning for others, whatever that means. We have family jokes that leave outsiders puzzled, and current cultural references are frequently meaningful only to members of that subworld, say the young, or to an older generation, or to citizens of a particular country.

We can't always say whether we will understand assertions we see on the page: reading Kant may be initially baffling, for example. Statements about the Good or the Beautiful may well be or have been meaningful to some people even if not to us, or indeed nowadays to anyone. We all probably need an explanation to understand the issues of Medieval scholastic philosophy, whether Christian or Muslim, and religion classes of whatever sort presuppose that we will find things baffling if left to our own devices. Indeed, pre-Reformation Christianity took this as given: don't read the Scripture, have the priest explain it to you. Nor do we necessarily know whom to turn to for explanation—if we feel we need one. (An ear pull or Hmmm may not need an explanation.) Do we ask a priest? Professor? What department? Mom? And we may try to figure things out ourselves that others can tell us about easily. Maybe there is a specific tool we don't know about that does things far more easily than what we are using or have rigged up. We should have asked in the hardware store!

Before everyone had Google maps or a car GPS, the joke was that men would never ask for directions and always get lost. It was ascribed to the male unwillingness to assume a subordinate position with another male—or worse, female. However, many things others have figured out cannot in fact be transmitted to those who don't know them because the process of figuring them out is the job of the individual. Dad can give Son advice about women (which may or may not be true or helpful) but Son has to be pro-active himself. We can show our kids how to do a million things like eat and dress and plan homework or order flowers or greet people, but the most important things are probably left to each person: we can't live others' lives for them, and we shouldn't. It's their life; they do have to reinvent some wheels over and over.

Note

1 Weber, "The Scholar's Work," 17.

PART IV
Words in the World

13

FORM FOLLOWS FUNCTION

In *The Mirror and the Lamp*, M. H. Abrams summarized the neo-classical era that preceded the Romantic as an era that simply mirrored nature in words or other media, where the perceiver is imagined to be outside surrounded by the world. There's no particular distance that has to be overcome to access the world or nature; the link is in the artist's technique of the mirroring. The emphasis is still on the mirroring, not the person doing it. But the technique became formulaic (five-act Aristotelian unities tragedies, alexandrine verse, predictable rhyme schemes, acceptable subjects for painting). This was understandable, because for the neo-Classical era technique was simply the means, not the end. So there didn't seem to be any problem repeating it and no necessity to personalize it or, as the later Modernists held, "make it new." Ultimately, by the time of the Romantics, the technique had petrified and had come to seem confining. Hence the Romantic preference for technique more keyed to individual visions, Shakespearean violation of unities and combination of high and low, music keyed to words and literature rather than (say) sonata form, and so on.

The Romantic era, by contrast with the neo-Classical that preceded it, imagined the individual no longer in nature, but struggling to re-connect with it. Art was the connector, but great effort was required to achieve this connection, and technique had to be personalized to express this individual struggle, focusing on exceptional people in exceptional faces of nature: mountains, the raging sea. The victorious struggling individual was, according to Abrams, the lamp that illuminated and ultimately brought us back to nature. Without this exceptional individual, we remain unconnected.

The Modernists grew tired of all this struggle and the focus on the personality of the artist, as we ultimately grow tired of everything we know. They saw us not as outside by the raging ocean but rather, like Matthew Arnold in "Dover Beach," that eerily prescient Victorian poem, inside looking out a window at the sea which

DOI: 10.4324/9781003217688-17

112 Words in the World

had ceased to roar and had instead become plaintive. And Modernism was the era of focus on the window, not what is seen through it, on language, paint, tones, movements. It's no accident that linguistic philosophy, the consideration of a discrete manifold of words considered as separated signifiers, and the analysis of how words mean in all other contexts, flourished in the Modernist era.

Early Modernism still saw things through the window, but late Modernism pulled back further and confined itself to the window—which produced the caste of explainers and analysts in charge of telling us that we would never be able to get beyond the window and were forever trapped inside. But now we have grown tired of this focus on representation rather than what is represented, and on the claims of those who explain representation to us, those in charge (they say) of the window. The last turn of the Modernist screw is the focus on the perceiver who looks at (not through) the window. The late Modernist era can be summarized as the objective of the subjective, following on the Romantic era's subjective of the objective. It gave objectified voice to the subjective act of perceiving. The individual became general, and so expanded to fill the world. With the self-awareness of the act of perceiving in Postmodernism, the era was at an end.

But let's step back even before neo-Classicism. Our world began, most people still agree, with the Renaissance. (Foucault's view is that it begins with early Romanticism, which is also defensible as most of us don't have access to the classical world that was "re-born" in the fifteenth century south of the Alps.[1]) The world beginning with the Renaissance—and even more so beginning with Romanticism—is the celebration of the individual. We can take this legacy and at the same time acknowledge that the Modernist era ran it into the ground, leaving us no alternative but to pick up the pieces and start anew.

When we leave Modernism behind, the window doesn't disappear, it just blurs into irrelevance as we change focus to what is seen through it. We will still be inside, as indeed we were for all previous ages: each of us is trapped inside our body. We just won't focus on that fact; we can go back to existing in relation to the world. We don't need the neo-Classical mirror to give us nature, nor the genius of the Romantic artist, nor the priestly classes of Modernism to explain the complex linkages of self to world that Modernism produced. When we are beyond Modernism, we will need neither artists nor philosophers to show us the world, neither the genius of a small group of greats nor the analysis of scholars. The cult of genius disappears, as does the priestly caste of interpreters who dominated the late Modernist era. Each of us is sufficient unto him-, her-, or themself. Merely by living, we unite the separated elements of self and world.

The first thing we need to do to make this possible is to clear away the Modernist obsession with a separable manifold of verbal representations, the window we call words. Everything is in words, so words are the most important thing—right? The first part of this statement is true of what it's true of, such as academic subjects in the humanities and social sciences—though there are many things of which it is not true, such as sighs and personal preferences, which as a result are largely ignored by Modernism. But the second part of this statement is false. All we

Form Follows Function **113**

have to do to go beyond Modernism is to change the focus from the window to what lies beyond.

If we start with the spectrum of what we do and realize that words are constituent parts of it all, but themselves part of a spectrum of what we do, we see that they are part (but only part) of what humans are in the world—and of our various relationships to something outside us. Words encompass both of these and are part of a spectrum of possibilities of how the relationships are expressed. If we can place words back in their proper context in the world, we can move beyond Modernism. Words aren't necessary, and they're not the world. They are a tool that we humans use in various ways. If we see words as things picked up on occasion and for various purposes, we can shed the Modernist burden of thinking it necessary to focus on them in general terms. We're out of the woods of words.

***

"Form follows function," asserted pathbreaking architect Louis Sullivan, father of the skyscraper, in his essay "The Tall Office Building Artistically Considered."[2] He was referring to the way the external shape of a building was determined by what its interior was to be used for. The honeycomb of offices necessary for an industrializing America required a container, and because of the use of steel skeletons for buildings, that container could be space-efficiently tall for cities, and square to fit square cubicle-rooms, as well as city blocks. Later architects, including his disciple Frank Lloyd Wright, would expand Sullivan's concept to include the idea of functionality that wasn't merely interior, but a relationship with the building's surroundings. These ideas ultimately led, somewhat paradoxically, through Wright's snail-shell Guggenheim Museum on a square plot in New York, to buildings seen as stand-alone artworks and whose interior was almost irrelevant, such as Frank Gehry's later Bilbao Guggenheim.

So the use of this concept in architecture is variable, and its meaning is subject to interpretation. One venue where its application proves more immediately fruitful is an understanding of the place of words in the world. If we focus only on extant words, as Modernist linguistic philosophy does, we are unable to have a sense of how or why they came to be, and hence of their place in the larger scheme of things. Cut off from the speaking or writing, they are dead. Where did they come from? What were they before they were words? Why do these words exit our lips or form under our fingers rather than other words, or none at all? After all, all words are spoken or written by people.

Yet we do this by causing them to become words from the cloud behind them, a cloud that contains (or "contains"), in some unspecifiable cloud-form, extant words, yet-to-be-invented words, usages, yet-to-be-invented usages, silence, gestures, grimaces, and all the other actions we can evoke, words being merely one action among many—but how many, the point is precisely, we can't say. We can analyze after the fact, separating aspects that are all rolled into one in the moment of speaking, but only for that one thing and set of circumstances. And any attempt to say that one aspect of something we say is primary—say tone of voice or body language—won't necessarily hold valid for other utterances.

114 Words in the World

Saussure is the quintessential Modernist theoretician of language, seeing words as separate from the world and from the people who use them. His fundamental distinction was between the personal, language that is used by the individual (*parole*), and the collective seemingly (by contrast) objective language (such as English or French, *langue*). These of course are not completely unrelated: if enough individuals use language differently, *parole* can alter *langue*. But this is like turning a battleship: it takes time and lots of individuals. So Saussure's effect was to polarize words into (almost) absolutely personal and (almost) absolutely apersonal. Yet words are in fact a changing and much less polarized mixture of the two. And then by being uninterested in what a single person says, because alone one person can't change the collective, Saussure made what was left seem like an entity he could consider in analytic and quasi-scientific terms. And in the early twentieth century, everybody wanted to seem scientific.

Saussure's depersonalized view of language was fundamental to the twentieth century's analysis of an external manifold that, necessarily for analysis, stays still on the page to be analyzed, as personal usage does not. Saussure purified language of the reek of the human. He murdered to dissect, as Wordsworth had it. And philosophers of language were gleeful: finally something to analyze! Of course: the Modernist worldview with its focus on the means of expression created the caste of people to analyze those means. The academics whose existence depends on accepting the givens of Modernism will defend their disciplines as givens, which is how things seem to them. But in fact they are the children of an intellectual era that is now dying. The Modernist point of view is bought at the price of separating out as a duality, language on one side and world on the other, what is in fact a unified whole in the person using the words. We are the ones who create (not the right word) the language falling from our lips or unspooling on the page, as every extant text or utterance was similarly "created" by other human beings.

We interact with the world through words, other sounds, gestures, and facial movements, and by just sitting still. There is a reason for everything we say and do, whether its content is specific or general. With specific utterances, it's easier to see connections: we usually don't tell people to come to dinner unless we want them to come to dinner and dinner is ready. But even there, situations determine what we say. In my family I have learned to say this before dinner is actually ready, because it takes a while to get action. We also send the wedding invitations before the wedding. Other utterances begin to peel further away from clear circumstances. My asking my wife, with a specific accent and intonation, if she wants more tea is not a question about tea but an affectionate reference to a moment in a vacation, and hence just a sort of couple's re-connect, neither a question nor about tea.

A focus on function, why words are made to be as they are, rather than their form, what they are once produced and how they relate to other spoken or written words, would allow us to see them not as inexplicable facts but as logically connected to a manifold they presuppose and from which they come. This would take focus off the words themselves, where it has been for so long, and put it where it belongs, on the people who cause them to be written or uttered. As it is, we

Form Follows Function   115

misconceive the nature of words if we see them as the beginning of our analysis and consideration rather than what they are, the end of a vastly complicated process. Words are the tips of icebergs, and we ignore the iceberg underneath at our peril.

The turn to abstraction produced the Modernist view of language and words as an objectively extant manifold. In fact words, whether written or verbal, are human emissions that are formed by our lips or from fingers. They are like our bodily fluids. We create and extrude them; without people they are nothing. Words are not, despite the universally shared Modernist conception of them, merely a manifold that can be dissected; the orthodoxy among thinkers of the Modernist century has been that words in all their forms constitute an objective manifold that can be studied the way science studies the objective world. They don't, and it can't.

There is a world beyond Modernism. To show this, I aim to reverse Saussure's valence, making *parole* primary over *langue*. At least I hope to make clear the price we pay for remaining at the level of abstraction of *langue*, a price that, it becomes clearer with time, is no longer worth paying. This is so because if people are focused only on that level, they ignore all others, and there is too much happening on the level of particulars to ignore. (The practitioners of Modernism took Saussure's distinction as given because it served their needs and expressed the world the way they saw things. Similarly, in the world past Modernism, we can reject it because it does not express the way we see things.)

Because we're limited creatures, doing one thing means not doing almost all other things. When we spend our time on the abstract, we are failing to pay attention to the particular. And what we know about the abstract is only true of the particular insofar as this abstraction applies to it. We may know things about male mammals, or even homo sapiens. But this is science, and whether it applies to any given individual is unclear. Am I male because of chromosomes? Testicles?—nowadays we require neither to claim someone is male. The less scientific generalizations in the middle of the scale are intrinsically problematic, because the relationship between the abstract and the particular is even more unclear.

One of the interesting points of deconstructionism was the perfectly valid observation that a text, which by definition has come to be, is doing a precise thing by virtue of being individual, and so is failing to do countless other things, just as each individual person fails to be billions of others. The intellectual fireworks of some commentators therefore consisted in showing what was not done, or, given the specificity of this one thing, what other specific things this one echoed or derived from. But the point is a fairly obvious one.

Sure, I echo countless others, and fail to be like all the others; yet I am me, not anybody else. We will never run out of clever things to say if we start listing all the things a specific work is not and those it is similar to in varying degrees: the whole world, except this one thing, stands at our disposal. But this is a trivial point, not to mention a repetitive one. We can just concentrate on what a single text does do, as we can concentrate on what is true about a single person. Abstractions that involve

116 Words in the World

people (as science does not) are generalizations from individual human cases, which don't go anywhere. We create a Venn diagram of many individuals; the small area of overlap is the abstraction. What if we later find individuals without this overlap? We change the abstraction to include them. (Perhaps the group of men now includes people with a vagina.)

As Wole Soyinka observed, countering Senghor's notion of "négritude," a tiger does not express its "tigritude."[3] Similarly, a person does not need to express personness, just be. Words are personal; we cause them to come to be—though Modernism has chosen to see them as existing outside people, as it would have to, in order to make abstract statements about them. For Modernism, words are not the emanations of particular people in particular circumstances; rather they exist in a manifold external to us that we can choose from, like food in a cafeteria line seen from the perspective of the customer rather than the cooks. This allows us to make general statements, but it also strips many aspects of words: we speak of "statements" or "questions" rather than asking which, if either, a particular thing I said might have been, what my tone of voice was, whom I said it to, and how it relates to the things said and not said before and after.

Similarly, science strips the messy world of particularity—in fact, its goal is to do so. But that means it's always getting caught with parts of context attached. Science is a continuing struggle to abstract from a world that clings tenaciously to our abstractions. Science gives knowledge, when it does, because it is abstracted from the context of the world. As a result, we can never have science about individual people as individuals. And each of us is inside our own individuality. What is true about us as individuals can't be scientific—once again, not because we have (say) free will or mind rather than brain, but because, abstracted from particulars—the essence of science—it can't be about particular people, and every person is a particular person. The area in the center of the spectrum isn't making statements about things true of people's bodies or surroundings, which are independent of people as individuals. It makes statements about people seen as abstractions, and so they are always by definition provisional and tentative.

Under the Modernist aegis, the individual aspect of language that ties it to a situation has all but disappeared from consideration. And that leaves us with virtually nothing. When I say "Oh really?" what is my tone of voice? Excited? Bored? Do I, an American, affect a British accent? If so, what does this mean to me? To the person I am talking to? Is it a private joke? Is this my normal way of speaking? How long do I hesitate before saying it and in response to what? How quickly do I speak? Have I said it once or repeatedly? Is this anomalous for me? To whom to I say it? Could I have said the French equivalent, and if I could, why didn't I? Is this something I frequently say? Is it something I say only to one person so it's a sort of recurring joke? Is it a quote? If so, do I think the other person will understand it as such?

If we strip away all this particular context and consider the bare words (or worse, an abstraction of the words—for example: questions are constructed this and such a way, and what Roman Jakobson called phatic communication like ummm and "I see" functions this or that way), we lose almost all information about them. Which of these labels do we put on "Oh really?" in these circumstances? It looks like a question, maybe, but is it one? This level of abstraction about words is like defining cancer without ever asking whether particular people have it or not. It may be intellectually interesting, but it has little connection with the world.

If I can flip Saussure's valence from abstract to particular, we can focus once again on the innumerable instances of *parole*. The result won't be scientific, and it won't be academic. But it will offer a more nuanced and interesting view of words than the language philosophy of Modernism. The science-envying academic twentieth century cut people out of the analysis of words and their works and actions, because people don't sit still. Change, if it happens, comes from individuals. Sometimes they do what you expect, but sometimes not—this is not a metaphysical statement, but the fact of their being individuals rather than abstractions. They may argue with you telling them why they did X or Y, or said/wrote A or B. And it's not clear who will be right. (Freud by contrast exemplified and perhaps pioneered the quasi-scientific view of people that cuts the individual out of their own motives: Dr. Freud was always right, because abstractions were not individual. His conclusions were implied in his methodology.)

So words are chosen by individuals among many options (including no words at all) as specific actions, and thus intrinsically link the individual saying them to that person's world, which includes other people. Asking for a muffin may get you a muffin, depending on availability, your ability to pay, and your tone of voice, but it almost certainly won't get you a haircut—or a rubber tire, unless you mispronounce it or are speaking a language badly. Things like the situation and your tone of voice (and availability) may mean you don't get the muffin either. Giving a moue in answer to a question about whether you are going out may be a Yes or a No, depending on circumstances. And we choose what we say or write depending on the people we are talking or writing to and the situation we are in.

Thus John Searle's focus on what he called "speech acts" that, for example, in his view get you married, is blinkered, since every use of words is a speech or writing act.[4] And "I do" only gets you married if we specify that this is so, just the way we specify that writing your name in a certain place on a contract obligates you to certain things. Instead, we could make the formula that trips the wire a smile or a handshake, or a nod. Besides, if you laugh hysterically while saying "I do" and run away, you are unlikely to be considered married—certain usually unarticulated conditions have to be fulfilled. Even "speech acts" are defined by their circumstances, even if they are so made as to be more specific and more formulaic (to sign this document—which obligates you to this and this—press X on your keyboard).

Foucault, still hugely influential decades after his death, may at first glance seem an outlier in the Modernist withdrawal into the separate world of focus on the means of expression rather than on what is said. He and his disciples consider the world outside of words—but only to chronicle the nefarious effects of, and impute negative purposes to, the finished texts they, like virtually all in the Modernist

118 Words in the World

century, focus on. It makes professors in the humanities and social sciences feel powerful to think that written texts, their stock in trade, are what subdue others. So Foucault ended up being yet another example of focus on the extant work of words, rather than on the cloud from which they came. So too contemporary Marxists like Fredric Jameson, who (like me) rejects the "prison-house of language": Marxism is also based on abstractions rather than individuals, a social science view of people rather than a literary-theoretical, two versions of the same sensibility.

Essays such as this are at the other end of a scale of connection to the world from a phone text that says "Keys on table" or "Come down!" if in fact the keys are on the table, and the receiver of the text is in fact up and is being told to come down and can do so. If the recipient is in a commercial airline over which s/he has no control, it's not a command, but a joke—and maybe the sender doesn't know which. The scale goes from tightly connected to so loosely connected (as here) that it may not be initially clear what the connection is at all. But that doesn't mean there is no connection. The phone text, besides being briefer, is a specific key to a specific lock, or perhaps a specific lock in search of a specific key. It answers a specific question, or asks one, or says "hi." Or LOL. The person to whom it is addressed, unless it is a wrong number or a butt dial, knows what the situation is, and adds history and context to make it make sense. Thus the number of people who can make sense of a personal text of this sort is severely limited, perhaps to one.

A longer essay, as noted above, reverses the relative importance of these elements with respect to the brief phone text among intimates. It has to offer history and context as part of its very being. So it's bigger. It has to carve out a place for itself that more immediate utterances with a limited number of known recipients can presuppose. In exchange for this requirement to cast a larger net into the world, it is accessible to a much wider swath of readers than the phrase only intimates understand. This is the reason for the famous variability of interpretation of literary or philosophical texts. This is not a weakness of the text, it's a result of the kind of utterance it is and where it fits in a spectrum of utterances, further removed from "come down for dinner." What is lost in the essay is the immediacy of the connection to the world: more people can understand it, yes, but with a much diluted sense of what the point is, and how what is written fits into the world. And they may understand different things. That's why we usually read philosophy or more substantial literary texts in a class with a teacher who has to show us where and how to look for the point—or even show us what, at least according to their reading, it is. We almost never have to have somebody explain to us what "dinner is ready so come down" means—unless it's not from somebody in our house and we aren't upstairs—a wrong number, or a text that because of a technical glitch sends only days later. And in that case, we ignore or delete it.

Sending a text requires knowing a lot about the recipient. Writing an essay, by contrast, is like putting a message in a bottle and throwing it into the ocean: I have no idea who will pick it up and read it, or when. Or whether it will be read at all. But even so, I am not without any sense at all of likely readers. They are going to be intellectuals or academics, or people who dabble in these worlds. Too, they will probably be Westerners or Westernized, anglophone enough to read this, and (if it is read in the next few years) living in the early twenty-first century knowing the things people now typically know. Of course, if this should survive a century (or more!) and be read or translated out of the world it was written in and for, that will pose the kind of fill-in problems for future professors we deal with now in classes and annotated editions, assuming there are any professors around at that point and in those places.

Notes

1   Foucault, *The Order of Things*.
2   Sullivan, "The Tall Office Building Artistically Considered."
3   Soyinka, quoted in *Oxford Essential Quotations*, from *Time Magazine*, 17 November 1967.
4   Searle, *Speech Acts: An Essay in the Philosophy of Language*.

14

THE CLOUD

Words are conjured from the cloud by us in our situation in the world. We mold what we say and don't say, do and don't do, to our circumstances at every moment of every day. Words don't start life as auditory signals or on the page; they come to be. This means that one option for words is that they do not come to be at all, rather the way that an infinity of babies fail to be born every second: no egg, no semen, no parent = no baby, or the non-existent babies from the millions of sperm that failed to be first at the egg. Imagine the world if we never "bit our tongue," as we say—and I for one don't speak at all for hours when I drive alone, or read.

Does talking to the cat (or to ourselves, or to inanimate objects) count as spoken language? We could argue this either way—maybe the cat hears our tone of voice or the repeated sounds. Does a goldfish? This has nothing to do with Wittgenstein's faux-profound insistence that there is no such thing as private languages. This seems to outlaw some things we do, but instead it only says that nothing we do with words is private. Is made-up vocabulary between siblings a "private language"? At least for one other person this isn't private. What could this "private language" which doesn't exist be? The point is, it doesn't exist. Talking to ourself? To the goldfish? Cursing at a broken tool? We do these things. Are we to stop doing them? Do we need to actually have someone listening in who understands? Or just say there could be such a person? This is a gray area, and Wittgenstein was bent on eliminating the gray areas. That's his view of the world: black/white, either/or. Never both/and depending on circumstances.

But of course we can sympathize with his desire to make unclarity go away. Life would be so much simpler if it did. Thinking about things that look like "private languages" is like wasting time on arguing whether the tree that falls in the forest with no one around makes a sound. For birds? Beetles? A tape recorder? Just the possibility of a tape recorder? It all leaves us wondering, what was this private language thing Wittgenstein wanted to declare invalid? In fact, nobody can say,

DOI: 10.4324/9781003217688-18

least of all Wittgenstein. In the same spirit, he insisted that mental states didn't exist. He wanted to start with multi-person communication, not consider what could precede this, such as the cloud, or an alternative to it. It's that old Modernist denial of the individual: we start with the abstractions of the laboratory or the classroom, not with what these leave out.

The price of ignoring the cloud from which words come is that we fail to understand that everything we say—and the actions related to speech, such as silence, grimaces, grunts, shrugs, or cocking of eyebrows—makes up specific alternatives among many, and these in turn fit into the larger fabric of life. Not talking or writing, but rather doing other things, also relates to words: instead of continuing a conversation, we can go fix dinner. Words are separated out and considered alone without the things that surround them at the price of fundamentally misunderstanding how they function for the people whose lips and fingers cause them to come to be.

Starting with words rather than asking about the cloud is like analyzing vegetables by starting in the grocery store, without considering how they got there. It's possible to do this, as the mere existence of the linguistic philosophy of the twentieth century shows. Indeed, a photographic essay of a grocery produce section might well be beautiful: all those piles of gleaming, perfect waxed apples, the intense green of massed broccoli, the orange carrots in shiny plastic bags, the mist valves over the vegetables that many stores have installed spraying clouds of minuscule droplets every few minutes from above to keep things wet and beautiful! However, the farmers would object that they were being ignored if no notice at all was taken of what they, or the truckers, or the stock people, did to make this possible. And we are the farmers, the truckers, and the stock people. And so all of us should strenuously object. It seems all rather Marie Antoinette, thinking that these things grew this way, rather than being the result of sweat and a lot of people who remain unconsidered and unacknowledged. Yet that is the position of most academic enterprises in the humanities and social sciences these days, from literary theory to philosophy to sociology and anthropology. It's time to storm the Bastille!

In speaking and writing, we cause words to come to be—but from a realm where (in some sense) they already exist in some way, only do not exist really, not anyway as words. Yes, it's confusing, but it has to be because we are using words to talk about where words come from. Where do words come from before they are words, and what are they before they are words, if anything? This is where it becomes difficult to articulate things, since I am trying to use words to say what is behind words, not in them, and how these relate to things not words. The alternatives to words before they come to be are clearly not other extant words (and grimaces, etc.), as if we chose one option rather than another from a pull-down list.

The alternative to the words we actually utter, that actually come to be, includes what we might call non-existent words that did not come to be, at least not then. And it's not at all clear what non-existent words might mean: not just not-yet words but never words. Yet considering the cloud behind words means focusing on "non-extant words" and the alternatives to words, and things that we do rather

122   Words in the World

than use words but that fulfill something of the same function with others—and on nothing at all, when I am not impelled to speak. Only if we do this can we understand the way words fit into the world as one action among many, actions by humans.

It won't do to adopt Aristotle's almost-substantive notion of "potential" as opposed to "actual" as if these were comparable, the potential a sort of ghostly or unformed version of the actual, all ready to take off the mental shelf. Even less are there words before there are words. Stream of consciousness in literature is as artificial as what it strove to replace: people don't usually "say" words to themselves, usually not even in fragmentary form. Nor is there a substantial "consciousness" where all these unspoken things are paraded, like rushes for a yet-unedited movie. They aren't nothing before they are words, but they aren't words either. And "consciousness," like all words, is something that only occasionally comes to the fore as needed. Was it there all the time? Sure, but then so is everything else we can subsequently speak of, such as speaking of the absence of consciousness, or of something else entirely—such as talking now of a chocolate ice cream cone, a subject I may not have raised for months or even years.

Words create the world, sure, but it's at least partly a world outside of us, and we cause the words to come to be. It's contradictory, and it's a paradox, but that's the way things are. In the sense that pre-history is the time before writing, so pre-everything is the cloud behind words—which do not accrete, but are said, written, read, or heard sequentially. *We* say *in words* that the world has always (for example) existed, or that it will exist after our death. The fact that without words there is no (for example) objective world doesn't mean it isn't objective: we didn't need Heisenberg to point out that our actions to some degree create the outside world.

The problems of establishing this world outside ourselves are endemic to the entire scale I am sketching here. At least at the scientific end, we are (or try to be) aware of them: that's the very essence of conducting tests in a laboratory, away (we hope) from influence by reality. Yet even here we have problems that must be continually addressed, which is why the scientific standard is based on being able to reproduce results. Reproducing results isn't an essential condition for truth—someone may have gotten it right the first time—but it acts as a mechanism to convince others. If you only get the result once and can't somehow manage to get it again, it seems likely it was due to factors you are unaware of rather than the ones you were aware of. Of course, the converse isn't true—mere reproducibility of laboratory results in a laboratory doesn't mean we can apply these with no problem in the world. All laboratories are laboratories, so what works there won't necessarily work outside where we can't control the variables as well.

Everything that people do, from science to personal actions like making dinner, is on the same scale where process and results exist in varying proportions. This is so because it's living humans who do it all, so they have to have a reason for doing it and have to figure out how to do it. What varies is the amount of human striving held to define the action, though this is never zero. The scale ranges from almost all process and minimal results at the personal end of the scale, actions such

The Cloud 123

as cutting the grass or setting the table, to almost all results and minimal process at the scientific end where the personal aspect is minimized. Still, everything on the scale has some degree of the personal effort to do it, and some degree of the objective result.

Preferring vanilla to chocolate right now is the least about results (can't be verified, can't be reproduced) but it too has its degree of objectivity: I say it's true just of me right now, not the world forever. With science, the pretense for some was that it was completely impersonal, so thinkers such as Popper and Kuhn seemed to present a real attack. In fact, they are right that what we look for presupposes a goal we set (Kuhn, my re-formulation of his celebrated "paradigm shifts") and is never 100% certain (Popper). However, science, because it's at the end of the scale—if it is, and we can demote things like phrenology or Nazi racial science—is more about results than anything else. The fact that things are on the same scale doesn't mean that they are all alike—that science is nothing but personal preference, for example, any more than the houses of the three little pigs were equally effective at keeping the wolf out. And what's in the middle, the humanities and social sciences, are an ill-defined mixture of the personal and the objective. With these, we should at least be conscious of the fact that to a large degree, they are about the personal journey, and even when we reach what we thought was the objective destination, that is not necessarily fixed for others or under other circumstances, as we did what we could under the circumstances for the purposes we had in mind.

Science works with non-human entities. Still, it's humans who do this. Thus its personal aspect is not just in the scientists themselves (what are they looking for? How do they set about looking?), it's in the fact that others have to be convinced of the results. Getting acceptance for your theories takes a lot of work. You don't just assert, you prove. And that doesn't happen because you want it to happen. Still, the markers that people move on the scientific board are themselves non-human. Assertions in the middle part of the scale—the humanities and social sciences, which are about human things more objective than personal preferences and less objective than science about corpuscles or asteroids—are movements by people about markers that are human, at least to some degree. Thus agreement is by humans about things that are human, not about things outside us. So we have skin in the game here that we don't with science, and the ability to object based on the fact that we are what is being talked about. (If asteroids did science on asteroids, they would have the same problem.)

Failing to realize that generalizations by people about what people do are always more or less useless, precisely because people don't need abstractions about themselves to be people, leads to the abstractions taking on a life of their own and being endlessly repeated. There is no fundamental problem with being human, so we don't need to solve it. Trying to do so leads to people getting into ruts. Language philosophers tied themselves in knots trying to explain reference, which is our word for the relationship of words to the world. Wittgenstein's early failure to nail it down, going down the rabbit hole of states of affairs and absolute particulars, led

124 Words in the World

him and the next generation of language philosophers to throw up their hands and say language doesn't relate to the world, only to itself. But that's wrong too: the *Tractatus* is too crystalline, the *Investigations* too blurry.[1] In fact, words have always been the same contradictory relationship with we who make them and the world in which we live. Life itself doesn't make sense—we weren't, we are, then we aren't again, at least not like what we were. It just is. So too for how language functions between us and not-us, bridging subjective and objective.

The good news is that because we are alive, we don't need to understand any of this. We think, we talk, we eat, we walk—it's only when we don't walk, or can't think, or have difficulty eating, that we try to solve problems. We can solve particular problems, but our default is not to have problems at all, for most of us most of the time. This is so by definition: what is, is normal. Our lives inhabit us; they are like waves that course through our bodies and exit the other end, leaving a lifeless husk. I am not the author of my life, which is like the wave I surf. So of course I can only deal with specific issues, not fundamental ones.

Modernism had a specific way of seeing words that has run out of steam. We can't merely start with words as a given when so much of words is in the cloud from which they come to be. Yet this is what Modernism did, separating words from their context and considering them in a quasi-scientific way. Granted, it's all silent in the cloud, and personal, and lacks words to describe it (coming before words, after all), so philosophy—which assumes it can nail down unvarying objects to consider—doesn't have anything to work with in the cloud. So it doesn't.

I'm talking about something that we get further from the more we talk about it. In that, it admittedly echoes Wittgenstein's "that which can't be said" in the doorslam at the end of the *Tractatus*. But of course we can talk about it some, and in circuitous terms. Wittgenstein was far too black and white. And his door-slam didn't last too long, even for him: it seems we don't like closed doors and keep trying to open them. Wittgenstein's "stay away" notion of the mysterious in the *Tractatus*, what can't be said, is the Janus face of his too clear notion of the way we should talk. (In his later thought, he postulated clarity by starting his consideration with what he assumed was common group understanding of words.) I aim to dilute the contrast between clear and unclear, seeing all these as parts of the same spectrum.

Before continuing, an objection: what if we do what Fleming suggests and simply abandon all the lovely scientific-sounding conclusions we have gained by considering language as if in a laboratory, bereft of its particular circumstances and focusing only on the abstractions that result from our point of view? Isn't this a loss of knowledge? It's certainly a loss of what it's a loss of, but the point is that (a) in losing this we open the possibility of considering other things, which is a gain, so the two balance out, and (b) what we lose isn't necessary to being human. It may be knowledge, sure (the laboratory results were what they were, say), but the fact that something is knowledge doesn't mean we should spend time with it.

There is plenty of knowledge in the world that doesn't help anybody: fingerprints of my first grade classmates, the bend of each blade of grass on my lawn, my thoughts over every moment of every day. Even Andy Warhol's night-long stationary camera shot movie, ironically (?) entitled *Empire*, of the lights going off and on in the Empire State Building (with a long dark period of many hours in the middle) is only one night, not ten years, or even one year—and nobody watches the whole thing. We have to pick what knowledge to pursue based on external reasons—that's Weber's point that what individual people want to do creates the study of what the larger structure ends up doing. We choose to pursue Topic X rather than Topic Y, or nothing at all.

Words come from the cloud. Authors and even casual speakers cause the words to come to be, and they are "chosen" from countless other things that never come to be, in a sort of bank we hold to some degree in common with others and to some degree not. The individual aims words at a target that is invisible to all but the speaker/writer: there, we say, I said what I "meant" to say. Or we just say it, we don't comment that it's the right word or phrase or what we "meant" to say. I hit the target that nobody but me knew I was aiming at; perhaps I didn't know what it was either, but I know when I hit it and when I miss.

That's where Wittgenstein's vilification of mental states finds some validity. In fact, I only say I "intended" to say X if in fact I said Y instead and go back to correct myself, or if someone else questions X. When I say X and have the sense of a bull's eye, I typically don't add that I "intended" to say what in fact I said. I said it, after all. Intention hasn't separated out. The cloth we are weaving hasn't hit a snag. Sometimes mental states aren't there, because we hit the target and we don't need to separate them from the action. Most of the time, probably. But sometimes they are, as when we need them to explain a mismatch with what happens that only I can see. If Wittgenstein "meant" that I don't ever see a mismatch between what happened and what I "wanted" or "intended" to happen (possible to say this only after the fact), he was wrong.

The thrust of Gilbert Ryle's influential anti-Cartesian position in *The Concept of Mind* is to change the way we talk, and to attack, along with Wittgenstein, anything that isn't accessible by others, insisting that what we have taken as evidence of another realm than the body in space is nothing of the kind, only a way of describing what is done where others can be aware of it. My notion of the cloud is certainly fuzzier than the well-ordered mind-machine (the "ghost") that Ryle rejects, but it more than what is left when Ryle and Wittgenstein are done demolishing the notion that there is anything that is not visible actions. It's perhaps paradoxical to say—and therefore make public—that we sometimes say that there were or are things at work which are not public. But we do it anyway, and doing so is not any more a "category mistake" (as Ryle held) than speaking of what we can't speak of, or of a place where we are not.

Ryle, like the positivists, wants us to stop *saying* X and Y (talking about the mind as something separate from the body), not to stop *doing* (or for that matter begin doing) Z. His point, in best Modernist fashion, is about words. We are not to speak of the mind as if it were a world like the physical world, a separable if otherwise congruent Janus face. Sure. But it's not nothing. We can in fact speak in

126 Words in the World

words about what lies behind words—we just can't be too precise about it. If all there is, is actions in the world, we can't say what allows me to write these words. The proof is in the pudding—this is Ryle's point too with the mind—but if we take away acknowledging that somebody made the pudding, we are once again in high Modernism, as well as unable to say how I can continue to keep revising this essay—or start it to begin with. Or know to say, "Good morning."

There is much to like about Ryle's insistence that people are not machines—not even, as he says, "ghost-ridden machines." They are people and cannot be described in mechanistic fashion. But he threw out the baby with the bathwater in using this anti-mechanism—which I share because it resists denying the fact of the individual case that cannot be codified—to insist that there was no mind separable from body: there is separable something, even if not a mind describable in the same sort of terms as body. We sense (not right word) an opening of a specific shape and attempt to fill it: usually we get it pretty much right, but sometimes a little wrong and sometimes a lot wrong. Oops, we say, that came out wrong. Let me try again! Or we say: He's surprised. Corrected to: no, he's flabbergasted. Or: I like you. Corrected to: I like you a lot. Or: The galaxy is X light years away. Corrected to: At least that's what my data show—how about yours? John is a horrible person. Or at least a very annoying one. Or maybe I'm just in a bad mood today? The possibility of correcting ourselves is proof of the cloud.

The fact that we can't nail down in words how the cloud functions doesn't mean it isn't there. It's not strange or creepy merely because it can't be put into words, at least not any more than things like a pre- or afterlife, or the meaning of existence, or what makes us human, which we've been talking about, and around, forever. We come to be and then we aren't. How does this make sense? We're the ones talking and trying to make sense of it. We simply weren't before, and at some point will cease to be. Huh?

No, it doesn't make sense—how do we know what makes sense and doesn't? Not by rules. The fact is, we do. If I started writing here about the GNP of China it would be out of place and "not make sense," unless I found a way after the fact to tie it in. How do I know I have proven my point, or whether I need more support? How can I edit this paragraph by adding, deleting, and re-arranging? In re-reading this essay I've found sentences that seemed abrupt or puzzling, so I had to provide corrections or explanations. What allows me to do this? We can't say. We can't explain the ability to stay or track or veer off in an argument either, any more than we can explain the process of steering through the cloud to "find" the right word with the right tone of voice in the right language (or decide to talk rather than remain silent). But that's the way it is. The cloud behind words isn't any weirder than what stands behind our thought or writing processes, or knowing/deciding what actions are appropriate with others. In fact, these are part of what defines the cloud.

Of course, it's a contradiction to use words to give a name (the cloud) to what words presuppose, but what else are we going to use? The difficulty of a thinker like Kant is precisely in his inventing tortuous not-white not-black neologisms to express something that can't be expressed in words at all. This tortuous complexity shows why we should resist the temptation to go beyond vagueness: the vagueness of "the cloud" is the point. We postulate the cloud of words that are not so much stillborn as simply never came to be, the way that the children of the millions of sperm that don't make it to the egg simply never are. If we don't do this, we can't explain why certain things do come to be among so many that could have been.

We are all the mothers of our words: they form within us, and we cause them to come to be, albeit sometimes instantaneously and without our being aware of the process. And they can be aborted: we decide not to say X or Y after all. Indeed, starting with extant words is akin to seeing women as the passive conduits for the man's child that must be formed within her, and all of us as "Handmaids" from Margaret Atwood's novel of a dystopia where the function of women is merely to serve as gestation chambers.[2]

In fact, there is nothing passive about this process: we make our words as they exit from our mouths or come out under our fingers (can this statement be verified?). We are not merely the petri dishes of words; we actively cause them to come to be—albeit from knowledge we have at least partially learned from others. And we can use what we know to invent new words, new expressions, new turns of phrase: to veer off the path, we have to know where the path is. And it's not as if we say words to ourselves silently and then out loud. They come to be in the process of coming out of our mouth, like the golden egg out of the goose: kill the goose to see what's inside and you see only normal guts, not a cache of golden eggs, even of reduced size.

This is true even of things I am pretty confident can come out of my mouth. Let's take as an example French. I'd say of course I speak French. But how do I know this? Well, I could a week ago (?), or was it a month? A year? When was the last time I spoke French? But do I sense potential French words floating around as I write this? Non. I am doing what I am doing. I wouldn't say it's as substantial as saying I "believe" I can speak French today—I just don't think about it, any more than I'd say I can walk or get up from bed. Maybe I won't be able to. What a surprise! Is it even that I "assume" I can speak French? If that means I am not conscious of not being able to, sure. But I'm not thinking of any of this. Where is it? And this: what if I can speak French but doing so would blow my cover as a spy, or the situation is such that doing so would be doing a favor to somebody I don't want to do a favor to? There is no physical part of the brain that can be the source of this—I have to do the addition on the things I know to arrive at an action.

Even saying French is "inside" me or "potential" (rather than there is no French in my brain, as there is no Mandarin) is too absolute and denies the human element. And for that matter, what does it mean to be aware that there is no Mandarin? What causes me to not try to speak it? Knowledge? Fear? Pragmatism? Besides, languages are not either present or absent; there are variations. Surely over time some specialized words will disappear from my French vocabulary (I don't navigate as if I spoke Mandarin, but I do navigate knowing I speak German) if not

128 Words in the World

used, so in a sense the French I thought was still available isn't; what I can speak is a much simplified set of phrases and words. But the same is true in English. I forget technical terms. And even now I have trouble with birds and plants.

Late Wittgenstein "solved" this problem by only considering what came out of people's mouths. Only he solved nothing at all. Fine, there are no mental processes. But what can we conclude beyond the fact that the person has said or written X or Y? Have I shown I "speak English" if I can come up with "yo dude" or "want to buy my X, mister"? Or do I have to show mastery of sentences of (Henry) Jamesean complexity? We can conclude nothing at all, certainly not things we normally want to say, such as that I speak French but not Mandarin. Do I speak English if I can say "I don't speak English" and no more? We can't say what qualifies for a capability if we only look at what people do. But by the same token we can't nail down potentialities or capabilities either. This is what comes from the Modernist assumption that words can be considered apart from the person from whose cloud they come, the fundamental assumption of Wittgenstein at all stages of his career.

French isn't the only thing I may "assume" is there and discover not to be, or that I decide is inappropriate or desirable under these circumstances (speaking Spanish with the lawn guy establishes one set of relations I might want to avoid— or establish). Maybe I am used to speaking complex flowery sentences at length in language X or Y and have no reason to think I am unable to do that when I open my mouth. But somehow I just can't manage it. Or decide not to? Or don't want to? Let's say I haven't had a stroke (I may not know whether I have or not). Maybe it's years since I spoke (say) Italian? I'm just unwilling? I'm depressed? Haven't had my coffee yet? At any rate, let's say I clam up or falter. Is this due to lack of ability, or lack of desire, or a calculated decision? It turned out not to be true that I could or would produce these sentences. I can look for the explanation, but what I know here and now is that it isn't happening. I was wrong. I can't speak this way. For how long?

Similarly I'd say, if asked (only usually I am not asked and have no reason to say this) that of course I can do X reps at Y pounds of whatever weight room exercise—that curling with 45-pound dumbbells will be hard and get me perhaps seven reps with admittedly not perfect form, but 25 will be too light and too perfect. I'd say I can do 20–22 one-armed pushups on the right side and the same on the left, only I recently pulled something in my left shoulder and only got up to 15 the last time I tried that side. I didn't know. Or let's say I over-indulge and am so hung-over I am similarly incapacitated. I can therefore be wrong in saying I can do any one-armed pushups. Are they potential that can be made actual? Surely something less substantial than that, something I have to cause to come to be. Maybe I can, but give myself permission not to? Don't want to show off? You can locate the ability to do the pushups in my muscles but I have to decide to use the muscles. And where do you locate that ability as well as my decision to use it?

Because all language comes from the cloud, it is based on what we have to call (for lack of a better word) choice. What words do I use if any? What tone of

The Cloud **129**

voice? What body language? Smile/frown/neutral? And what language? Philosophy of language tends to assume a single language to eliminate the need for choice between them, let's say English or French or German (for Quine in "Two Dogmas of Empiricism," it's the language of the people who say "Gavagai" when pointing at a rabbit), and a single criterion of capability, usually "native speaker" level. But let's back up.

A view that ignores function and starts with form, taking extant words as the start and separating them out from what they are embedded in and the fact that people cause them to be from among many alternatives in the cloud, is forced into a sort of Zeno's paradox when confronted with the fact that they are something humans do for specific situations and reasons. We need to ask why words are the words they are and not others, and/or why words came to be at all. Of course we needn't do this, as philosophy of language has shown, or literary theory or philosophy that compares texts to texts without considering how or why they came to be. But if words are separated out, then every other step of the process can be too, and the arrow never gets to the target as every action can itself require a "choice" or a prior action.

What decides what language I speak in? I speak several, so I have to "choose" one. But which? Let's say I chose German ("I" "chose" "German"). How did I know to do that? How did I know where to go (in my brain? In my consciousness?) to find it? How did I know I had to go anywhere? How did I know it was a choice ("choice") that had to be made? What keeps "German" together as a bundle so that, if I choose, I can speak only German or only English? What allows me to unbundle it? How do I make the choice to speak only German rather than drifting between language? How do I know this is an option in these circumstances? What tone of voice do I use? How long do I go on? Do I use simple words or more complex? What body language? How do I know how to make my body (say) shrug? Why a shrug of precisely this duration and intensity? How do I do it? How do I make the decision not to (a) turn away in disgust and/or (b) smile condescendingly and/or (c) roll my eyes?

If we imagine a person (the "I") in the cab of a steam shovel as the analogy of "I" making choices, pulling certain levers to get certain actions, or the organist with busy hands and feet at the organ whose result is the music, we never get to action because we need to postulate the human that can transcend and blend together into a seamless whole the now increasingly fractured actions. The problem is that we have moved Cartesian dualism back a stage by separating out words as if they were self-subsistent entities. Instead of assuming life and asking how life works, we no longer assume that the arrow gets to the target at all: at every step the controller in the cab has to make another decision, another choice. Only of course they aren't decisions or choices because these are things the whole person does and we have separated the person out into constituent parts of cab and driver, organ and organist: if we do this we can't put them together again any more than Descartes could.

How about alternating languages? How many words of each? In what order? Only postulating a cloud before words can make this explicable. Je suis très content

130 Words in the World

to see you again especially here and now, e perché ich erst gestern an dich gedacht habe, lo sabes? (This is possible with people who also know several, indeed possible with anyone but only fun for someone who can follow me—but maybe not following me is the point? So what is? To impress and confuse?) What about mixed languages: Spanglish, Franglais? The "level" of words I use (scholarly, or slang, or somewhere in between)? My tone of voice (friendly or condescending or in between)? How do I know when and how to alter from one level or tone to another if I feel I have got it wrong or used one as much as I should? Should I tell a dirty joke, use a crude word for sex or a body part? How crude? How euphemistic? What "body language"?—as we call our shrugs, moues, intakes of breath, hangings of heads, and so on, in so many variations we can never list them all.

Modernist thinkers will ask things like this: What deep structure of language in general allows me to combine relevant parts of different languages into a sentence that is meaningful for someone who speaks all of these? This question is neither more nor less interesting than questions like these: What deep structure allows me to know I need to put more "warmth" into my tone of voice? What allows me to do it? What deep structure am I appealing to without knowing it when I hesitate a micro-second before I answer a question that may be uncomfortable (or am I hesitating to emphasize my answer?)? What deep structure impels me to make a "moue" gesture with my lips and open my eyes a fraction at this point in the conversation? What deep structure impels me to get up and leave in a huff? These are the same sorts of questions as questions about how we know how to make "meaningful" sentences. And sentences like mixed-language ones aren't meaningful to many people—and maybe some of the other sentences in this essay aren't meaningful to some people either. "Meaningful" isn't a quality of the sentences themselves, as language philosophers typically think. It's an invisible target the person from whose cloud the words come is aiming at.

Or this: What deep structure allows me to use words in a striking way, one that isn't technically correct but somehow fitting (we sometimes call this poetry)? For example, it's frequent now to appropriate Yeats's use of the verb "slouches" in his poem "The Second Coming." Literally, it means letting your shoulders droop and not standing up straight. But in the poem it's a "rough beast" that "slouches towards Bethlehem," so the verb "to slouch" seems to mean an ugly, ungainly, and off-kilter means of locomotion. I've seen this used in numerous newspaper headlines: slouching towards a political compromise, for example. It ain't pretty and it ain't fast and/or direct, though the general direction is clear. But for sure it's butt ugly.

Or Yeats's speaking of Leda in his poem of that name as being "overmastered by the brute blood of the air"—blood can't overmaster, and it isn't in the air. Only here it refers to Zeus metamorphosed into the shape of a swan who is in the process of raping Leda out of nowhere: she is stunned. The first words of the sonnet are these, as sudden for us as it all was for Leda: "A sudden blow." What deep structure is thus usage obedient to? Or is it a divergence from deep structure (if this is possible, which it shouldn't be if the structure is really deep)? But why these

The Cloud   131

divergences and not others? When may we diverge and when not? How far? In what direction? What if no one has ever seen this particular divergence before? How can we tell a good divergence from a silly or bad one? What is the deep structure of divergence from deep structure? Here Weber would warn us that no sociology can explain how Raphael painted the *Sistine Madonna*.

The fact that the alternative to words is always no words shows us, perhaps most fundamentally of all, that there is a world behind or before (the metaphor can vary) words that are written or spoken; we can't take them for granted because sometimes we don't produce them at all, and silence is part of life too. Failure to speak or nod to someone we know (what the eighteenth century called "cutting someone dead") is its own statement. If you insult me, one option is for me to turn away, or simply to stand silently. Words rather than no words is not a given. So we can't start the film rolling when there are words.

Neither are the precise words I might write or utter a given, and iPhone texting has made written words much closer to spoken than they were in the era of lengthy letters and tracts. Instead, I might "aim at" some form of assent, but nothing dictates the precise expression I use. Something, therefore, stands behind my choice (for lack of a better word) of "OK" in a text or conversation when I might say—if I take from the English pile rather than French or German one, and it's appropriate for me to be somewhat looser/less high toned/youthful—"Great" or "Right on" or "Roger that" or type a thumbs-up emoji, as something stands behind my "choice" of assent. All I have to do is pick something from the "yes" pile rather than the "no," and there are many possibilities to pick from. There are also other piles—prevarication? Ambivalence? And they aren't even piles until I consider them as such.

How for that matter do I (or "I") choose (or "choose") assent (or "assent") as the bag from which I pull the precise words I use, the "yes" pile as the one I forage in? It might be better to indicate indifference. Or negativity, at least for now. Many precise facts determine the generic bag I take something from. And what does it mean to take something from a bag? What is doing the taking and from where, given that this is all me carrying out a relationship with others in the world? The only words we have are in the world, not definitory of it. Descartes speaking of the "I" was not presupposing what he set out to prove. Doing so is the inevitable result of our inability to describe the whole with parts.

Whom am I addressing? What effect do I wish to have? What is my history with this person/these people? Nor is "assent" a sort of Platonic Idea that can itself be nailed down as primary for this situation. That's the word I'd be inclined to use because the basic idea is yes rather than no, but perhaps a lag in responding verbally or to a text turns assent into something closer to refusal, "Yeeeeeees, well" in a text, and tone of voice in speaking. (What makes me "inclined to use" one word or the other?) Frequently what I say doesn't matter; it's the fact that I say anything at all. Or that I say something pleasant rather than unpleasant. Or in a specific language. The purpose of "making conversation" is not to learn things or transmit information, it's to say formulaic things in a group that offend no one and establish a human connection—or simply pass the time.

132 Words in the World

These all show us that what is, the words we use, has many unseen alternatives: I can perhaps even say after the fact which ones would also have fit the circumstances, and how well, and which sort of, and which not at all. Or whether something besides words, say smiling silence, or turning disgustedly away, would have worked better or just as well. Or not go back over alternatives at all. Language philosophy is unable to answer how I (or "I") navigate among these possibilities that may not be possibilities at all—the pre-uttered. Even opponents of abortion mean the fetus when they speak of the "unborn child," not the children that didn't happen because another egg or another sperm was there at the decisive moment.

Any analysis of anything, here language, of necessity uses what for the circumstances are more abstract concepts that can apply to many particular situations. However, the distinction between particular and abstract is connected to the circumstances under which the abstraction was coined or reached. Thinking we could tell by looking at the utterance whether it is particular or abstract was Wittgenstein's mistake in the *Tractatus*. Tone of voice is abstract when compared to the words "I hate you"—vituperative? Loving? But it is precise when compared to "aspects of language utterance." And tone of voice means nothing if we don't know the history of these people. Is this a new thing for Person X to have said in this way? Is it an ongoing joke? Is it a surprise to the other person? Is it an assertion that falls on a scale where others should or should not respond? A literary reference? Both?

In Edward Albee's *Who's Afraid of Virginia Woolf?*, Martha comes into the apartment and says, "What a dump." It turns out to be a quote from a movie she can't quite remember—and she and George, her frenemy husband, have a discussion about whether Bette Davis said it, and how. In the Mike Nichols movie of the same name that stars Elizabeth Taylor and Richard Burton, Taylor says it with a Bette Davis intonation and a sweeping gesture of one hand. They would have seen the earlier movie together and her husband would have gotten the reference—or not?

Everything we say both implies and fits into everything we know and everything that is the case with the people we are speaking or writing to. Things can be misunderstood, but we can be aware of this, try to prevent it, and try to rectify it, if we are still there or can come back. (If we are dead, or have moved on, we can't.) And there are different levels of my knowledge about the people I am talking to as well. The people I live with every day have the history of our shared experiences and what we have all said, which I may be able to evoke with a single word or gesture, or which may be assumed. And perhaps I am quoting something or referring to something in our history with the same words that would be incomprehensible to others.

Notes

1 Wittgenstein, *Philosophical Investigations*.
2 Atwood, *The Handmaid's Tale*.

15

CIRCUMSTANCES

We're always where we are and who we are; to some degree we determine this and to some degree not. Nature/nurture/effort/headwinds or following winds, etc., etc., etc. But more to the point, all discussions of the elements that we can discuss and change or not change, and to what degree of each, presuppose the situation. We have to bring these up. Otherwise we just are. This doesn't mean we only discuss what affects us personally right here right now: a young person can investigate the effects of ageing, a smart person can investigate the effects of being less gifted, a person with a skin color that is prized can investigate the situation of the less fortunate. Or the reverse. So motivation for moving to abstractions can vary. But each of us is in a situation that we can articulate as needed or desired, but which is the starting point of where we are. This can change—we get older, we get heavier, we change our situation in the world. We can be aware of these changes or not aware—and if not aware, can become so as we make mistakes and note people's responses. But at every moment we draw breath, our default seems zero to us: we are who we are, we are where we are. Since we're boats floating on the surface of water, no matter how high or low the water is (and extremes of these can create problems), we are always on the surface. We float, and that is our point of departure. There has to be a reason for getting abstract on this situation to question it, figure it out, or try to change it. The default is not questions and words, but no questions, no words.

I sit here now typing. I have to think: I am 66. My run this morning was good. I weigh 195 lbs. I am married. My wife is out on a hike with a friend. My sons are both here because my wife picked my older son up from college two days ago. My younger son is still asleep. It's Sunday morning. I just clipped the cat's claws with my older son. It's 2020. The election has happened but Trump is still making noise. We all wonder what he will do after.

In a movie about Iris Murdoch called simply *Iris*, Judi Dench, playing Murdoch, begins to show the effects of Alzheimer's. To find out how much is left, the doctor

DOI: 10.4324/9781003217688-19

134 Words in the World

asks: Who's the prime minister? Dench/Murdoch knows that one cold. Blair, she says curtly, Tony Blair. Similarly, if asked, I can tell you the answers to comparable questions, and a lot more. How old am I? I know. How much do I weigh? I can tell you. Where does my mother live? My mother-in-law? All that. What is French for "I don't care?" There are several. What was the grocery store like just now? (Full.) But the names of all my first-grade classmates? (I know some still, actually. But all?) The plot of a specific Balzac novel? (The famous ones, OK. But there are so many!) Who sent us a certain kitchen gadget as a present? Hmmm. If I don't have a reason to answer any of these questions, I don't. I'm just here, typing away. Everything that I do or say or think is precise. Even thinking and doing—before we bring these actions front and center, they are in the cloud. We are at zero, then things are brought out or come out from the cloud.

Can we get more basic than specifics about people? No, because then they become specifics too. (Only non-human scientific facts transcend the fact of our humanness, and this by design.) We can ask what it means to float, maybe whether and how fast we are drifting—but these facts are givens as the result of being alive. And being alive is the thing we cannot fundamentally understand, as it is the pre-condition for everything else. We are given something initially as the result of life, and can question this or make it specific, or try to change it—as individual actions, not as the givens of life. We can't say more about Life, which is inexplicable—only precise things that it makes possible. These precise things are in words.

Words come from the cloud but are shaped by the world as they come to be. When we do speak or write, what we say/write is keyed to circumstances—or we have problems. The supermarket checkout lady doesn't know me, but she can tell I'm a normal person so far as she knows, am giving her a smile, perhaps am wearing a cool coat (as I did one day—buckskin fringe), and am not buying weird things. So I can talk about checkout type things—big crowd today, came in for one thing and look what I got!, don't these flowers look pretty?—or maybe I have seen her before and can say that she's been working here a while, and how long is it? I don't talk about Rwanda, or ask about her personal life. And we all have a sense of what's appropriate, what we can and cannot say.

Or most of us do, at any rate. Failing to understand circumstances leads to problems. Eliza Doolittle, from George Bernard Shaw's play *Pygmalion* and the subsequent Lerner and Lowe musical *My Fair Lady*, was taught to speak only of the weather and everyone's health. Her mistake when taken into society was thinking that the rain in Spain was weather rather than a verbal exercise to get her to say long "a" correctly, and not realizing that her aunt dying of influenza, while health, was not appropriate. And the joke on Shaw's part is that her audience keys to her perfect pronunciation and clothes as well as the fact that she's a guest of a wealthy woman (the professor's mother, doing her son a favor) to assume that she has to be merely proficient in a new sort of "small talk" slang. The idea that she is merely an out-of-her-depth flower girl with a perfect accent is so outlandish it never occurs to anyone. And they're not wrong to think this way. They are using the signals they have learned: outlandish exceptions remain outlandish.

All utterances are particular to those uttering them and both imply and encapsulate relationships between the speaker/writer, the world, and other people. These can be about the galaxy or the bloodstream, or about whether we are having a good day or prefer chocolate or vanilla. But these different sorts of relations to others and the world (and to the self) determine how these utterances are received and reacted to by others. Words fit into specific configurations of the world—for lack of a better term for "everything."

Wittgenstein said, at the opening of the *Tractatus*, "The world is all that is actual," in my translation. In most translations this is usually turned into an assertion about assertions—"all that is the case"—*die Welt ist alles, was der Fall ist* (1). But he should have added, also what isn't the case, or actual, because we can make them so: Wittgenstein postulated a static world without people to make it come to be.

Words also cause these actual facts to come to be as they articulate these —perhaps wrongly, so that we correct them, understanding that we have gotten the words wrong. The world is both inside and outside words. To some extent, words create the world, in the sense that words are parts of the world, and written history (in words) starts with writing. But because both alternatives of what we call realism (words mirror the world) and linguistic idealism (words create the world) are in words, then of course both are true, not one or the other alone.

All of us situate ourselves in the world, which is the surface of the water. And this determines what we say and do, or don't say/don't do. I navigate in my house and car as if I weighed 195 lbs, and am 6'2"—because I do and am, but only rarely think about these facts. I don't navigate as if I were 5' and 120 lbs. I live my life as a man, we might say, though I am only sporadically aware of being male. I go to my office or bedroom because I know it's mine. I go to the right place in my house to find my books, or a specific book. I look for the eggs in the refrigerator, not the garage, and cook them on the stove, not the washer. I would know if suddenly there were a strange person in the house. At the grocery store, I act as if I am at the grocery store, and do not act as if I am in the swimming pool. And so on.

These things are guardrails I am not conscious of that guide my actions, including my production of words. Collectively we call these "situational awareness" because actually we can't explain them—what situation? And surely I'm not always "aware" that I am mid-60s and married, it's just that I don't do things as if I were 19 and unmarried. Or that I speak X languages. Awareness of any of these is a sometime thing, called forth from the cloud under specific circumstances. These guardrails can disappear, and I can be wrong about them. So are we people using words? Or river banks through which water flows? Perhaps the latter, though because we are the banks, we can to some degree control the direction and speed of the water. "Choice" isn't right to describe the passage of words from non-being to being, because in any instant we are acting out of "situational awareness," which seems far more submerged than hesitation or head-scratching. Yet this phrase is no more satisfying. What situation? And are we aware of it?

136 Words in the World

It doesn't seem to be choice when we see somebody we like and spontaneously smile, advance with our hand out, with "Hello!" or "How are you?!" on our lips. Instead, it's more like the way water flows between the banks of a river—it had to be this way. Only of course it didn't. What if the situation is that we see this person across the room at a meeting? We would do and say none of these things. At most we'd smile slightly if we can catch their eye, then turn back to business. What if this is someone we are having or had an affair with and s/he is there with his/her partner who knows nothing about it? At most we might hold a glance for a micro-second longer before looking away. That situation and that history make a different set of river banks for the water to flow in. So too the fact that, say, the affair had been acrimonious at the end, or so long ago we no longer wish to acknowledge it. We create many such riverbanks in quick succession—did we come on too strong? Or maybe the other person is responding in kind? We dial up or back (as we say metaphorically, also speaking of warmth or coldness of response, equally metaphorically) depending on what's happening and our desired result—which itself can change in microseconds.

Language is like a magic act for others who watch, where we conjure words, specific words, with a specific purpose, responding to specific situation. To them it looks as if these come from thin air. But for us they don't.

All of a sudden, when you come upon it, this essay, paragraph, or sentence is there before you. To you it seems as solid as a rock, but to me it's hitting a target that only I intuit. I don't see what I'm aiming at yet; I merely sense (?) it in a vague way. I couldn't have spent months on this, writing, re-writing, arranging, adding, and crossing out if I didn't have a target that grew clearer through the process of writing. You didn't see the target; I felt it vaguely at the beginning when I started to write, and it came into focus in the same act of aiming and hitting it. That's a paradox, but that's the way words work. No wonder Modernism just cut off the person aiming at the partially seen target half-lost in fog, and started things with the bull's eye. It's all far easier that way.

We know that this cloud from which language comes is not nothing, because it produces utterances—specific utterances. But it's private. At the same time, it contains possibilities that are defined by others, and takes the form it does because of a situation in the world. We can try to articulate the cloud for any specific past utterance(s) but we can't articulate the whole cloud—what lets us articulate this new thing. We can shine the light into the darkness and illuminate specific things, but we cannot make the darkness go away, because it's behind us as we stand there holding the light.

I fit what I say into an as-yet unspecified hole that (here's the paradox) takes shape as I move my words into it, each forming each. I can say that things I or others say or write are wrong, or insufficient, and that saying something or not saying something fits this particular situation, and what it will be or not be. I can tailor what I say (or don't) to what I know or do not know about my auditor(s) or reader(s): how much do I have to fill in or explain? I can also say when I have misspoken or made a mistake, and have to apologize and/or correct myself. All that

Circumstances 137

is based on a relationship with the world. And I can react to others as well: do they make sense? Are they presumptuous/long-winded/aggressive? There is no rule book to consult to answer these questions: they come from the cloud, and the cloud is linked to us and to the world.

We have to make the decision to move forward from silence to words, much as we make the decision to start running on our daily jog or exercise: the body is comfortable just sitting there, so this requires a decision on our part, or at least an impetus. If we are sitting deep in thought, or just sitting, and someone addresses us, we have to put things in a new gear to answer. If we're the one who starts speaking, it's still a rupture of silence, such as when we walk into a room with our hand outstretched saying, "How do you do?" For written things nobody has asked us for, such as this, the initial impetus is like a shooting star that streaks across our thoughts. I am more conscious of there having been something, the residue, rather than of what it is, and when I sit down to write, I start with this something, a momentary spark—intuition? And months or even years later, there are dozens if not hundreds of pages, each word of which has been chosen among many others and revised many times. But it's all part of the construction of the same essay, during which time I have done dozens of other things, including eating, sleeping, working out, defecating, setting the table, and brushing the cat, to name just a few. How could I do that? If words are considered as extant things, this question cannot be answered. But if we consider them as things I/we do, what's odd about that? In a minute I will stop typing and go make more coffee. And then come back.

In the case of this essay, the initial itch I am scratching here, the initial impetus to write, was the realization in the middle of the night that an idea in my last essay had been only fleetingly considered and not developed. In the context of that essay, this would have been too much, making a sort of bulge in what otherwise was a fairly sleek shape, taking too much attention off the main subject. This idea was the realization that postulating things like societies or cultures is the result of a prior intuition (right word?) that creates a space that they fill, a target that they hit. Concepts are born for a reason: individuals birth them under specific circumstances, and for specific reasons.

We aim at something we define only in the reaching of it. But isn't that life? To set out with vague goals that become precise and usually change in the process of achieving (or missing) them? Nothing changes for me if Chomsky or Kant articulates abstractions: I'm not everybody. I'm an individual, and I'm moving in the world of actions, I'm not just an instantiation of an abstraction. Again: this says nothing about whether people are free or controlled. If we can articulate both as poles on a spectrum, then of course both are true and what varies is only where we are on the scale at any given time and in any given set of circumstances. There's no gotcha in saying, Fleming is actually expressing his subjective POV! That's the point, or part of it. And that's the part that the twentieth century—Modernism and its focus on the finished work rather than on asking where it came from, and its insistence that words have meaning only through relations with other words—has overlooked.

138   Words in the World

Individual people use words; books are written by people, for other people, in their common world. To understand writing (or speech), therefore, we need to understand not their subjective nature as opposed to their apparent objectivity (that's Nietzsche), but rather the fact that words are themselves behind our distinction between objective and subjective—a distinction the subjective self makes by using words in an objective world. And something that is neither wholly subjective nor wholly objective stands behind words, the unseen manifold from which they are conjured up by our mouths and fingers—or rather, by us.

Words come from the cloud behind them, the cloud inside each of us that is the source both of our individuality and of our commonality. It's counter-productive to define it further, as that makes it precise and hence places it within the world again, where it is merely one alternative among many. We should merely gesture at it—that's Wittgenstein again, who had many good impulses. It's what all words presuppose, which is why I resist the impulse to write elaborate formulae on the classroom computer or chalk board, or to invent impressive new phrases for philosophy students to puzzle over. (Wittgenstein grew weak at the point of truth tables: so scientific!) The impulse to make the ineffable precise is, however, I admit, strong. It makes us feel so powerful and authoritative! Like priests conjuring the gods! In fact, we're just people using words.

16

WHAT IS THE SELF?

Much ink is spilled nowadays on the question of whether there is such a thing as the mind rather than merely the brain, some ineffable personal entity that Ryle mocked as the "ghost in the machine." Is AI the same as human intelligence? Can machines think? And so on. But form follows function: our words are produced by the circumstances we are using them for. If we abstract out a specific function from people, rather than considering the cloud that allows all functions, then of course it is possible that a machine can do it. Such as filling boxes of crackers. Or tightening screws on a car assembly line. The more defined the action, the clearer it is that a machine can do it.

But something like tightening screws is only at one end of a scale that becomes progressively more difficult for us (NB: for *us*) to summarize simply, or at all. The unanswerable question, can a machine think?, is simply postulating the end of the scale as the end (nothing is more inclusive than "thought") and asking whether we will be able to make a machine that not only can inch up the scale of complexity but also reach the theoretical end point. But of course we can't say, because we never see that far; all we can do is move slowly in the direction of increasing complexity. We can't jump to the end, because we can't ever define the end, and we can define machines.

So this is not an issue of essence, whether being human is something only humans can be (I'd say sure, and why is that a problem?—only a bird can be a bird, it can't be a dog and certainly not a desk or a bottle). It's the difference between defined and undefined. Machines are defined; "thinking" isn't. All we can say is that in theory we can make more and more complex machines—made of more and more specifics. This probably means that fewer and fewer people understand them. As Weber observes, we don't even understand how the streetcar works— most of us, anyway. Can we make a machine so complex that nobody will understand it? Well, if it's a machine, somebody made it, right? So somebody has

DOI: 10.4324/9781003217688-20

140 Words in the World

to understand it, even if not us. Or are we asking if we can create Frankenstein's monster, something that transcends our specificity, that isn't merely the sum of all our specifics? Well, lots of babies are born every day, so I suppose the answer is yes. But can we construct one?

Why is this question so important? People used to dream of flying like birds, but we accept a metal cylinder with stationary wings, propelled by fuel, as "flying." Thus we accepted that something we understand can be what we had dreamed of, which means something we didn't understand. The issue is not whether we can play God, it's that being what we are, human, we can't see beyond our own bubble, and that is defined from within the line, not from outside. Thinking is at the end of the human scale as seen from within by humans.

So can machines think? If we can define what we mean by this, then of course this is possible, if not now then at some point. If not—something approaching the cloud, no. It's our cloud, not the machine's. Can a machine have a cloud? Maybe, if it's a machine considering machines. But we'll never know, because we're always people considering people, as well as machines.

The problem with the cloud is that we can't be aware of it except in ourselves, so what we see from a really sophisticated machine is identical to what we see from another person—but only if we focus on that one thing. Let's say we have a machine that can play tennis. But can it get distracted and smile at somebody on the sidelines? Let's say yes, we added that feature. Then add 100 other things—precise actions or functions—people can also do: the machines will be developed to include them. Then come another 100 things people can do. We can try to make machines that include these. But there are another 100, and another, and another. The machines always play catch up to people. If we want more people, just have more babies.

The mind vs. brain issue is a live one for our day, but we humans have created it. What we're trying to do is to see beyond the limits of our own personhood— make the large and imprecise small and precise. We understand machines, but we can't ever understand thinking (or consciousness, or any of the other terms we use to refer to the "everything" of being human). So if a machine (that we understand) can do what we do, that means we can understand what we do as well. We're really trying to nail down people, not ask about machines. It's another form of trying to give Most Fundamental Rules for being alive rather than accepting that we will never understand.

What other people ("other minds") produce looks just the same as what machines produce—from which some philosophers have concluded that we have no access to other minds. Perhaps not, but we have our own—which doesn't mean, pace Descartes, that we can access it, because when we access it, it externalizes, changes shape into the contents of the world. Articulation makes the cloud precipitate. It's no longer cloud. This is Heisenberg before Heisenberg—or rather, it's always been true, and not more so of atoms than of ourselves. Why have we failed to realize it?

All those mental states Wittgenstein declared nonexistent in the *Philosophical Investigations* are really just part of the cloud that are ancillary to the language, sort

What Is the Self? **141**

of like propulsion for the missile, and we only haul them from the personal cloud when we have difficulties in the social realm. Wittgenstein was right that they don't always become the focus of our attention—and only gain a place in our consideration when we haul them out of the darkness. But that's when they do exist. And the fact that we can haul them out means they are not nothing before—potentiality? Even that sounds too substantial. They weren't and now they are. We make them come to be, but that means they came from a somewhere that we can't name until we do.

That's certainly odd. Not to mention not scientific. But why should it be odd that language itself is odd? I don't say "mysterious," because that is too associated with the Realm That Cannot Speak Its Name of Wittgenstein. (NB: see how I was able to consider a target and then fail to actually aim at it? Most of the time this action goes unarticulated, perhaps so fast I am not aware of it—I instinctively choose the path I choose.) It's part of life, and life itself is odd. We come to be and then aren't, we bring certain things to the game—only here's the odd part: we don't know what they are and only find out by playing. We accumulate knowledge, and then it's all dissipated when we die. We live with other creatures we seek to communicate with, but it's always something of a crap shoot whether we end up doing this or not. We learn from other people who will never know we have learned from them. Or how about the strange action of making new creatures like ourselves from inside our bodies, or for that matter consuming other living things, whether plants or animals, that allow us to consume yet others, produce other creatures like us, and then leave all of it, memories of us fading for the next wave of people and all but gone for the next who, if they remember our name or have a few of our possessions, think that these tiny crumbs are who we were. Why should it seem any stranger that language is odd than that life itself is so? Or any less strange?

We're always part of this process (that was the realization of the phenomenologists): we can't get behind it (they thought the thrownness was getting behind the process). This means we can't give form to what allows this process to happen—or rather, we do for a time, then it solidifies as a position and somebody tries to get behind even that. That is, so long as there are individuals, human life. We never solve all problems for all time; we never get at what allows us to continue to try. Wittgenstein seemed to be at this place in the *Tractatus* 7: what can't be said has to be left in silence. My evocation of the "cloud" is Wittgensteinian in spirit: a gesture to something we can never attain. We can't articulate or reason about what allows us to articulate and reason. We can't ever codify what allow us to say things like these: He proved his point/didn't prove his point; this needs more evidence; you've beaten your argument dead; you're saying the same thing over and over; this paragraph doesn't belong here; you've skipped a step; this doesn't fit. Yet we do all these things all the time, and I have done them countless times in writing this essay.

Thus the mind/brain conflict. Related to this is: what unifies the self? The short answer is, nothing, because if we put a finite label on this, it becomes only part of

142 Words in the World

the whole it is supposed to unify, not the whole. Nothing unifies it, because the self is everything—including all things outside of it that the self perceives, thinks about, and postulates. And somehow we function! In fact, the notion of the unified self is circular: things go OK, so I must be unified. Maybe they just go as they go, and no "I" is unified at all. Maybe an ununified "I" is also the nature of who we are. Whatever we say about the self, the opposite also has to be true, because we mean the self as something behind everything—and that we can never attain.

Consider this, as a sort of sum-up of what it means to be alive in the world.

I am walking down a path. It is a path I have walked hundreds of times over 33 years. It is the path leading to the main building at the US Naval Academy. I have seen the shadows of these trees in winter countless times, sometimes with a few identically clad students, sometimes without. I know where I am going—to the main gym. I went to this gym for decades before switching to another one, but now I am back. To the right and left are squares of grass that are alive with memories for me, if I were to pursue them: this is where my daughter and then my two sons looked for Easter eggs every Easter. I've been in the building in front of me many times. I will walk straight ahead and then turn left across the terrace to enter the gym at the second floor, giving me one more floor to go rather than two if I had entered at ground level. There will be a few students now at 11 am but not many. I will do a quick full-body workout and then leave, all without even changing. It's Friday.

I can't say I am conscious of these things. Rather I can pull them up. Or I assume I can. Only I don't know what it means to assume. Only last week I found myself astonished that a recent photograph of my wife was, she insisted, from December: somehow in my mind, with the mild weather we'd been having, I was ready to say it was fall—September or October maybe. Sometimes I find myself in the kitchen where I have walked saying, Now what did I come in here for? What makes it that I see these late winter grass patches with the overlayer of memories? That I know I am going somewhere I have been before? For someone like Proust, it's the fact that they're all up there and can be called up, or pop up spontaneously, as I get random scenes with my dead brother or his dissertation advisor, whom I visited repeatedly in her nursing home after her multiple strokes, watching her go progressively downhill to death.

I know a lot of things that I know (assume?) to be there in the shelves of my mind ready to be taken off the shelf and dusted off. They certainly aren't front and center. And in fact I am not thinking about them as I walk. Reading Balzac. The beach hotel in Gisenyi, Rwanda. The brief affair I had with a woman in Paris. What shoes I am wearing. If somebody asks me about any of these, I can answer. But I don't know beforehand what I will be able to say. Maybe I will try to talk about Balzac and find my remembrance of *Le Lys dans la Vallée* gone—so I change the subject, or remain general. If I'm still in school and there's a quiz, I flunk it. A book I read thirty years ago isn't something I can talk about for any great period of time, but one from last week may be. Do I remember where I am going or am I letting habit drift me? Probably I am just walking, because I am sure (meaning

What Is the Self?   143

what?) that I will remember where I am going when I get to the building. Or is it that I am engaged in the larger project of walking to this gym and so don't need to think about it?

When I am in the car driving, I am really paying attention to the Brahms Double Concerto that has just come on the radio until a car coming up on my tail causes me to think about the road. Was I completely oblivious to it before? To the point that if someone told me I was driving a car I would have contradicted them? Of course not. How is it that I suddenly remember I forgot to mail the letter I had meant to put in the mailbox? It's unrelated to anything around me. Maybe I wonder if the old lady who goes walking at about this time will be out. Maybe I am angry at something one of my teenaged sons did.

Do I know where I'm driving? Do I know what shoes I have on? Socks? Underwear? Certainly if I think about it I can say because of recent memories—maybe I don't remember what underwear, but I had to choose the socks, orange and green, to go with the jacket. I know where I am driving. Only maybe not. At the end of this road there are several options for where I might go: Washington, Baltimore, Naval Academy, or my sons' school. Sometimes when I am not thinking, I go as if to the Naval Academy when I should be going to the school. And sometimes I say, I have to stop talking and concentrate on where I'm going. Once I choose, say, Baltimore, I have to think about whether I am going to go on MLK Boulevard to Johns Hopkins, where I go to concerts, or whether I want to continue on Russell to Pratt and then Charles as I do when I am going to the Walters.

Sometimes things aren't on the shelves of my mind at all. I blank out (as we say) on somebody's name or a construction or word in (say) Spanish—I am agile enough that I can substitute something else that is usually acceptable, just as when, in French, I can't remember (say) the imperfect subjective I re-phrase midway to something less complex. I can't remember all Balzac titles so if I am talking about Balzac I might say "works like *Lost Illusions or The Lily of the Valley.*" Or if the subject is Maupassant, what was the name of the novel set in the spa? Gone. If that is the question I am asked, I have to say I don't remember, but if I am speaking more generally about Maupassant I can talk about how affected I was by *Une Vie/ A Life.* But even not remembering such precise things is normal. It's even normal to lose one's train of thought completely, if it's not too often. Now what was I saying? And the other reminds us what we were talking about, so we can almost always pick up the discourse and go on. I am pretty sure I can run intervals, because I did it yesterday and I know my body doesn't degrade that fast. But what if I sprained my ankle? I don't know if I can run on it until I try. I was revved up a week ago and spouting voluble Italian—how about now when I'm tired? I don't know.

And there are Descartes-level errors in my memories, my perceptions. Sometimes we don't know what these are. The whole recovered memory movement of the 1990s, now thoroughly discredited, where adults encouraged people to visualize things they believed they had experienced as children—horrific scenes of sexual exploitation in day care centers, most notably—stands as an example of false memories. Science fiction loves the conceit of implanted memories: we believe they are ours, but why? Because we can recall them. But what if there is another reason we can recall them? And then there are the people who "remember" being Cleopatra, or whoever. (It's suspicious that virtually no one remembers being a nameless slave building the pyramids. But BTW why is this suspicious? What law or rule does this contravene? It's our sense that individuals always decide theory in favor of themselves as individuals.) We can make mistakes in memory just the way we can make mistakes in grammar. Mistakes are part of the tapestry. Still I'd say, mistakes aside, and science fiction aside, what I remember are my memories; what I can recall is what I perceived. I am I. That's not more unified than disparate. It's just the way things are.

WORKS CITED

Abrams, M. H. *The Mirror and the Lamp: Romantic Theory and the Critical Tradition*. Oxford: Oxford University Press, 1953.

Albee, Edward. *Who's Afraid of Virginia Woolf?* New York: Atheneum, 1962.

Allen, Woody, director. *Love and Death*. 1975. United Artists.

Arendt, Hannah. *The Life of the Mind*. New York: Mariner, 1981.

Arnold, Matthew. "The Study of Poetry." Preface to *The English Poets*, edited by T. H. Ward. London: Macmillan, 1880.

Atwood, Margaret. *The Handmaid's Tale*. Toronto: McClelland and Stewart, 1985.

Brunetière, Ferdinand. *L'évolution des genres dans l'histoire de la littérature*. Paris: Hachette, 1890.

Camus, Albert. *L'Etranger*. Paris: Gallimard, 1942.

Curtiz, Michael, director. *Casablanca*. 1942. Warner.

Dewey, John. *Art as Experience* [1934]. New York: Perigee, 1980.

Eyre, Richard, director. *Iris*. 2001. Miramax.

Foucault, Michel, *History of Sexuality Vol. I: An Introduction* [l'historire de la sexualité: La volonté de savoir, 1976]. New York: Vintage, 1980.

Foucault, Michel, *The Order of Things: An Archeology of the Human Sciences* [Les mots et les choses: Une archéologie des sciences humaines, 1966]. New York: Pantheon, 1970.

Frye, Northrop. *Anatomy of Criticism: Four Essays*. Princeton, NJ: Princeton University Press, 1957.

Geertz, Clifford, *The Interpretation of Cultures*. New York: Basic, 1973.

Hawkes, Howard, director. *The Big Sleep*. 1946. Warner.

Hegel, Georg Wilhelm Friedrich, *The Phenomenology of Spirit* [Phenomenologie des Geistes, 1807]. Translated by A.V. Miller. Oxford: Clarendon Press, 1977.

Heidegger, Martin. *Being and Time* [Sein und Zeit, 1927]. Translated by John Macquarrie and Edward Robinson. New York: HarperCollins, 1972.

Jameson, Fredric. *The Prison-House of Language: A Critical Account of Structuralism and Russian Formalism*. Princeton, NJ: Princeton University Press, 1975.

Kuhn, Thomas. *The Structure of Scientific Revolutions*. Chicago: University of Chicago Press, 1962.

146 Works Cited

Lang, Fritz, director. *Metropolis*. 1927. Universum.

Lévi-Strauss, Claude. *Structural Anthropology* [Anthropologie structurale, 1958]. Translated by C. Jacobson and B. G. Schoepf. New York: Basic, 1963.

McNeill, William H. *Plagues and Peoples*. New York: Anchor, 1973.

Mann, Thomas. *Death in Venice* [Der Tod in Venedig, 1912]. New York: Knopf, 1925.

Marcuse, Herbert. "Repressive Tolerance" [1965]. In Robert Paul Wolff, Barrington Moore, Jr., and Herbert Marcuse, *A Critique of Pure Tolerance*. 95–137. Boston: Beacon Press, 1969.

Miller, Arthur. *Death of a Salesman*. New York: Viking, 1949.

Nichols, Mike, director. *Who's Afraid of Virginia Woolf?*. 1966. Warner.

Pinker, Stephen. *The Language Instinct: How the Mind Creates Language*. New York: William Morrow, 1994.

Polanski, Roman, director. *Repulsion*. 1965. Tekli-Compton.

Popper, Karl. *The Logic of Scientific Discovery* [Logik der Forschung, 1934]. London: Hutchison, 1959.

Quine, Willard Van Orman. "Two Dogmas of Empiricism." In *From a Logical Point of View: Nine Logico-Philosophical Essays*. 20–46. 3rd ed. Cambridge, MA: Harvard University Press, 1980.

Rawls, John. *A Theory of Justice*. Cambridge, MA: Harvard University Press, 1971.

Ryle, Gilbert. *The Concept of Mind*. London: Hutchinson, 1949.

Sagan, Carl. *The Demon-Haunted World: Science as a Candle in the Dark*. New York: Random House, 1995.

Saussure, Ferdinand de. *Course in General Linguistics* [Cours de Linguistique Générale]. Ed. Charles Bally and Albert Sechehaye, 1916. Translated by Wade Baskin. New York: The Philosophical Society, 1959.

Searle, John. *Speech Acts: An Essay in the Philosophy of Language*. Cambridge: Cambridge University Press, 1969.

Shklovsky, Victor. "Art as Technique." In *Russian Formalist Criticism: Four Essays*, edited by Lee T. Lemon and Marion J. Reis. 3–24. Lincoln, NE: University of Nebraska Press, 1965.

Soyinka, Wole. Quoted in *Oxford Essential Quotations*, 4th ed, edited by Susan Ratcliffe. From *Time Magazine*, 17 November 1967. Oxford: Oxford University Press, 2016. Also: www.oxfordreference.com/view/10.1093/oi/authority.20110803100227485.

Sullivan, Louis. "The Tall Office Building Artistically Considered" [Originally in *Lippincott's Magazine*, 1896]. ocw.mit.edu/courses/architecture/4–205-analysis-of-contemporary-architecture-fall-2009/readings/MIT4_205F09_Sullivan.pdf.

Veblen, Thorstein. *The Theory of the Leisure Class: An Economic Study of Institutions*. New York: Macmillan, 1899.

Warhol, Andy, director. *Empire*. 1964. Warhol Films.

Weber, Max. *Ancient Judaism*. Translated by Hans H. Gerth and Don Martindale. New York: Free Press, 1952.

Weber, Max. "Basic Sociological Concepts" (First chapter of *Wissenschaft und Gesellschaft*). Translated by Keith Tribe. In *The Essential Max Weber*, 311–358. Abingdon: Routledge.

Weber, Max. *Economy and Society: An Outline of Interpretive Sociology*. Edited by Guenther Roth and Claus Wittich. New York: Bedminister Press, 1968.

Weber, Max. *The Essential Max Weber: A Reader*. Edited by Sam Whimster. Abingdon: Routledge, 2004.

Weber, Max. "Introduction to the Economic Ethics of World Religions." In *The Essential Max Weber*. 55–80. Abingdon: Routledge, 2004.

Weber, Max. "The 'Objectivity' of Knowledge in Social Science and Social Policy." [From *Gesammelte Aftsätze zur Wissenschaftslehre*, 1922]. In *The Essential Max Weber*. 359–404. Translated by Keith Tribe. Abingdon: Routledge, 2004.

Weber, Max. *The Protestant Ethic and the Spirit of Capitalism* [Die Protestantische Ethik und der Geist des Kapitalismus, 1905]. Revised 1920 edition. Oxford: Oxford University Press, 2010.

Weber, Max. *The Religion of China: Confucianism and Taoism.* [Konfuzianismus und Taoismus, 1915]. New York: Free Press, 1951.

Weber, Max. *The Religion of India: The Sociology of Hinduism and Buddhism* [Hinduismus und Buddhismus, 1916]. New York: Free Press, 1958.

Weber, Max. "The Religions of Civilization and Their Attitude to the World" [Last chapter of *The Sociology of Religion*]. In *The Essential Max Weber*. Translation by Sam Whimster. 81–100. Abingdon: Routledge, 2004.

Weber, Max. "The Scholar's Work." In *Charisma and Disenchantment: The Vocation Lectures.* Ed. Paul Reitter and Chad Wellmon. 1–42. New York: New York Review, 2020.

Weber, Max. *The Sociology of Religion.* Translated by Ephraim Fischoff. Introduction by Talcott Parsons. Boston: Beacon Press, 1964.

Wilder, Billy, director. *Sunset Boulevard.* 1950. Paramount.

Wittgenstein, Ludwig. *Philosophical Investigations* [Philosophische Untersuchungen]. Translated by G. E. M. Anscombe. Oxford: Blackwell, 1953.

Wittgenstein, Ludwig. *Tractatus Logico-Philosophicus.* Edited and translated by David Pears and Brian McGuinness. Introduction by Bertrand Russell. London: Routledge, 1961.

Woolf, Virginia. "A Mark on the Wall." In *Monday or Tuesday: Eight Stories.* 47–54. New York: Dover, 2011.

INDEX

Abramovic, M. 26
Abrams, M. H. 17, 111
Addams, C. 80
Albee, E. 132
Allen, Woody 90
anthropology 27–28
Arendt, H. 90
Aristotle 122; tragic hero 30
Arnold, M. 40; "Dover Beach" 111
artificial intelligence 139
Atwood, M. 127
Austen, J. 32, 86

Bacon, F. 60
baloney busters 78
Baltimore Museum of Art 38
Balzac, H. de 142–143
Barnes Foundation 37–38
Benjamin, W. 20
Berkeley, G. 92
Berlin, I. 80–81
"Big Sleep, The" 108
Bligh, Capt. 64
Bocaccio, G. 12
Bogart, H. 108
Braque, G. 35
Breker, A. 22
Brunetière, F. 15
Buddhism 39, 90
Burton, R. 132

Cambrian explosion 65
Camus, A. 15

Carroll, L. 107
Casablanca 19
Chomsky, N. 97
Christianity 13, 77, 90
Christo 40
comparative literature 25
Conan Doyle, Sir A. 56
Cone Collection 38
Concept of Mind, The 125
Covid-19 6, 8, 15, 37
cultural studies 25

Darwin, C. 47, 100
David Copperfield 32
Davis, B. 137
Death in Venice 40
Decameron 12
Defoe, D. 15
"Demoiselles d'Avignon" 37
Dench, J. 133
Deneuve, C. 24
Derrida J. 4, 11, 20, 25, 57–59
Descartes R. 88, 92–93, 131, 140, 143;
    doubt 45, 96; dualism 129
Desmond, N. 5
Dewey, J. 37
Dickens, C. 32, 86
Dr. Seuss 95

East Germany 24
Ecclesiastes 59
Eliot, G. 45
Eliot, T. S. 26

Index 149

Emerson, R. W. 62, 98
evolutionary determinism 51
Expressionism, German 22

Faulkner, W. 20
Faust 31
Feminism 60–61
Fontana, L. 35
Foucault, M. 4, 25, 39, 67, 117–118;
    homosexuality 14; modern age
    15–16, 112; oppression 18, 27;
    power 20, 57
Frankfurt School 22, 67
Freud, S. 47–48, 56, 58, 82, 92, 117
Frye, N. 88

Galileo 55
Geertz, C. 11, 28, 57
Gehry, F. 113
Gibbon, E. 13
Goethe, J. W. von 25, 31, 82, 105
Gorey, Edward 80
"Guernica" 37

Hegel G. W. F. 28–29, 105
Heidegger, M. 20, 66
Heisenberg uncertainty principle 103,
    122, 140
Hinduism 90
Hirshhorn Museum 40
Hitler, A. 22
Hobbes, T. 42, 80
Holmes, S. 56
Hopkins, G. M. 79
Hubble telescope 54
Hume, D. 54, 66–67, 78, 99; *Enquiry*
    47–48

Identity politics 5, 7, 18–19, 76
Iris 133
Islam 90

James, H. 128
James, W. 52
Jameson, F. 3, 118
Jakobson, R. 67
Jefferson, T. 39
Johns, J. 35
Joyce, J. 7, 61
Judaism 90
Judd, D. 35

Kant, I. 29, 47–48, 78, 91, 97, 126–127;
    Critique of Pure Reason 88–89, 101
Kuhn, T. 6, 15, 123

Laforgue, J. 26
Lang, F. 6
Lawrence, D. H. 22
Lee, Peggy 9
Leeuwenhoek, A. van 54
Lévi-Strauss, C. 58, 88
Leviticus 90
logical positivism 52, 54, 58, 90, 99,
    103, 105
Louis, M. 35
Louvre Museum 38

McNeill, W. 13–14
Malinowski, B. 27, 57
Mann, T. 40
Marcuse, H. 61
Marx, K. 4, 6, 29, 48–49, 58, 82–83;
    class 20; expansion of capitalism 18;
    ham-fisted 94, 101
Matisse, H. 35, 37–38
Maupassant G. de 143
Mead, M. 27
Michelangelo 85
Miller, A. 30
miracles 50
Mirror and the Lamp, The 17, 111
Modern Language Association 20, 25
Mondrian, P. 4
Munch, E. 80
Murdoch, I. 133
Museé d'Orsay 37
Museum of Modern Art New York 37
Musil, R. 61
Mussolini, B. 81
My Fair Lady 134
Myron 85

National Museum of the American Indian 28
New Criticism 4, 20
Newton, Sir I. 55
Nichols, M. 132
Nietzsche, F. 17, 39, 138

Occam's Razor 101
Orwell, G. 7

Picasso. P. 37
Polanski, R. 24
Pollock, J. 35
Popper K. 54 92, 99, 123
Pound, E. 61
Pride and Prejudice 32
Proust, M. 61, 80, 83, 142
psychology 26–27
Pygmalion 134

150 Index

Quine, W. van O. 129
Qur'an 90

Reinhardt, A. 35
Rembrandt van R. 38, 59
Repulsion 24
Rocky (Balboa) 38
Rothko, M. 35
Russell, B.29
Ryle, G. 125–126, 139

Sagan, C. 28
Said, E. 20, 28
St. John's College 86
Sartre, J-P. 20, 82, 104
Saussure, F. de 29, 59, 114–15, 117
Schoenberg, A. 7
Scholasticism 20–21
Searle, J. 117
semiotics 4, 20
Senghor, L. 116
Shakespeare, W. 32, 111
Shaw, G. B. 134
Shelley, P. B. 61
Shklovsky, V. 4, 61
Shroud of Turin 76
Smith, D. 35
social contract theorists 80
sociology 27, 66
Soyinka, Wole 16
Stalin, J. 81
stream of consciousness 20, 122
Stein, G. 22, 38, 57, 61, 98, 107
Still, C. 35
structuralism 4, 11, 20, 25
Sunset Boulevard 5
Sullivan, L. 113
Swan Lake 83

Taylor, E. 132
Thatcher, M. 75
Theory of the Leisure Class, The 27
trolley problem 91
Twitter 67

Unitarianism 90
United States Naval Academy 86, 142
University of Chicago 102
University of Virginia 39

Veblen, T. 27
visionary art 45
Vonnegut, K. 13

Warhol, A. 59, 125
Weber. M. 51–52, 57, 106, 139; personal
    aspect of sociology 31, 75; religion 27,
    39; "The Scholar's Work" 58, 82; Sistine
    Madonna 49, 102, 131; spirit of
    capitalism 11–12
Whitman, W. 31
Wilder, B. 5
Wittgenstein, L. 81, 89, 97, 105, 107,
    128; mental states 125, 140; mysterious
    141; *Philosophical Investigations* 124,
    140–141; private languages 120–121;
    Tractatus 13, 65, 89, 124, 132,
    135, 124
Wodehouse, P. G. 74
Woolf, V. 132
Wordsworth, W. 114
Wright, F. L. 117

Yeats, W. B. 130
Yertle the Turtle 95

Zeno's paradox 129

Printed in the United States
by Baker & Taylor Publisher Services